ADAPT

ADAPT

A leader's guide to staying relevant and being
recognised in the digital age

LUÍS GONÇALVES
Foreword by José Pedro Pinto

R^e think

First published in Great Britain in 2021
by Rethink Press (www.rethinkpress.com)

© Copyright Luís Gonçalves

Contents

Foreword

Those of us with leading roles already understand that our businesses, whatever sector we're in, are changing fast. Transformation is not new for most of the companies that have seen reasonable success over the past few years. Most leaders and teams are already familiar with the need to evolve and continuously seek improvement through lean management.

It is, however, clear that the digital age presents new and multidimensional challenges for all of us. Boosted by digital, customer expectations and behaviours are changing at an incredible pace. To adapt and become more agile, companies are compelled to change their day-to-day processes, even their values and, ultimately, their culture.

Although it may appear overwhelming, digital transformation conveys tremendous opportunities, as described in this book. More than ever, dramatic improvements of customer experience with innovative journeys in (and across) different channels are within reach. It has become easier to access new markets, faster and at a lower cost. New tools enable us to better understand client needs. Higher automation with artificial intelligence allows optimised service levels, more efficient business models and, consequently, increased competitiveness. And – no less important – working in this new environment can be a lot more fun.

Perhaps you have already felt an urgent need to transform your business but you don't know where to start. Or maybe the results from the changes implemented through your marketing strategy and in your organisation are insufficient. In that case, this is a great book for you. It proposes a structured and global approach to enable your business to reach its full potential, whether it's a startup or a large multinational.

When I met Luís Gonçalves, the first thing that struck me was his passion and drive to challenge the status quo. In *ADAPT*, he presents his impressive knowledge of multiple markets and a comprehensive methodology, illustrated with practical examples from his own experience as a consultant or an employee.

There is no question that any structural change in an organisation must be sponsored by that organsation's leaders. It is their responsibility to acknowledge the need to move forward. This book will provide the necessary guidance for you to better understand how digital is disrupting your market and inspire you to accelerate the journey of transforming your business, so that you can embrace change with confidence. As Luís Gonçalves explains, there will be frequent obstacles along the way, but if you remain persistent, and allow your teams to express their ideas and talent, united by a common vision, solutions will naturally appear.

It's time for action.

José Pedro Pinto
Chief Marketing and Sales Officer
BNP Paribas Personal Finance (Portugal)

Introduction

When the Covid-19 pandemic struck in 2020, life suddenly changed. The norms we took for granted were turned upside down and inside out. Humanity's instinct for survival, however, meant that we wouldn't be beaten. As lockdown took hold across the globe, families and business found new ways to adapt in order to connect and survive. It was a catalyst for enforced change. Unfortunately, many long-established businesses, large and small, were ill-prepared to withstand the effects of the pandemic. They were effectively shipwrecked. Those that did survive are now operating in a world changed beyond recognition, clinging to the wreckage in the hope that the tide will carry them back to a place of safety and security.

As catastrophic as Covid-19 has been, the digital age storm has been gathering strength since the beginning of the century, disrupting at ever-increasing velocity how businesses and customers navigate the high seas of commerce. The risk to many traditional businesses that were founded on 'industrial age' models is apparent: unless they embrace the urgent need to stop and adapt, they will soon sink without trace.

With the unexpected, sudden arrival of Covid-19 a new sense of urgency to create change arose. The time for comfortable complacency and reliance on the old ways of conducting business is over. The 'new normal' has arrived with a bang and it's here to stay. It's also here for us all to take full advantage of in any way we can. Businesses must adapt if they want to survive, and this survival depends entirely upon business leaders being the centre of the transformation. Their survival success is predicated on them driving this transformation forward and owning it, not delegating it to others without any sense of meaningful involvement. With that in mind, I wrote this book during the 2020 quarantine to collate all the ideas and practices that I've worked with into a clear and concise methodology. I want to help executive leaders of organisations, both small and large, consider how they can adapt their businesses to the digital age and what steps they need to take to achieve that transformation.

Before the pandemic, many long-established, traditionally run businesses seemed content to coast.

Indeed, for many, having gradually recovered from the global financial crisis of 2008, they'd performed admirably well in the turbulent economic conditions which were beginning to boom again. It was easy to turn a blind eye to the threat that lurked beneath the shallow waters and an 'out of sight, out of mind' mindset didn't seem harmful. It obviated any real need to take a close look at the world around them. Despite a host of disruptive competitors in their niche cropping up at alarming rates and some slackening off in footfall and/or turnover, as long as they were generating enough cash flow to attract more credit or make enough profit to keep them afloat, there was surely still room for their products and services in the marketplace? A bookstore that could offer a personal, ambient customer experience with sofas, armchairs and a friendly barista had a competitive advantage over a behemoth like Amazon and customers could only visit a hairstylist in person, so it was impossible for digital competitors to muscle in on their patch, but Covid-19 stripped away many of these advantages.

The reality is that even before the pandemic, a multi-national online grocery retailer managed to sell hair products in the millions, whereas the hairstylists' stock sat on their display shelves for months at a time. This situation needs to change. I want to share my vision to help business owners and executives become relevant, to build fantastic organisations that make more money, create more jobs, and impact the economy so that they can help their employees and families enjoy a better quality of life. They can only achieve this if they adapt and implement digital transformation right across their business. I realise that the term 'digital transformation' may send cold shivers down the spine of many executives in the belief that it's either irrelevant, or a job for their IT experts. My aim in this book is to present a persuasive argument that such a change is necessary and that only by being at the heart of it will success be truly successful.

While the effects of Covid-19 might gradually recede, the digital era will not. It's not simply another new-fangled project mired in technical jargon – it's an overarching mindset, one in which newly established competitors are investing in ever-increasing numbers. If we fail to acknowledge that the way business has been traditionally carried out over the last fifty, even thirty, years has dramatically and irrevocably changed, then our ability to thrive and survive in the new landscape will be severely diminished, to the point of extinction.

I've aimed this book specifically at executive leaders, managing directors or board members that are almost certainly already using a variety of digital assets such as accounting and sales software, online store fronts or simple data collection, but know they need to go that extra mile to make these assets work harder. On their own, these assets don't create a digital-era-fit business, they are simply functional and siloed in the same way as any traditional business assets.

In the following chapters I offer you the outline of a roadmap to help navigate the bumpy road ahead. The ideas I present are offered as opportunities to provoke thought and raise awareness of measures that can then be implemented in ways appropriate to your business or sector that it operates in. These apply to any business leader who is willing to drive that transformation with the aim of surviving in the digital era. The roadmap involves following, extracting and adopting many of the ideas outlined in the five pillars of my ADAPT Methodology:®

- **Approach:** Understanding how to acquire new customers in the digital era

- **Data:** Learning how to use your data to optimise your business and customer experience

- **Agility:** Recognising the need to build a company that can react and respond quickly to changes in the market

- **Product:** Developing and implementing a digital product strategy

- **Transformation:** Understanding why and how the entire organisation needs to change so that it can competitively thrive in the digital era

In the final two chapters I share my insights of how to avoid the common digital transformation mistakes that are easy to make, especially if you've never attempted anything like this before in your organisation. I also offer some guidelines of what characteristics to look for when you're considering hiring expert consultants to help you develop and implement your digital transformation. Knowing that your partners are exactly right for you is vital, and this could be one of the first decisions you will make in the driving seat of change.

Over the course of my career, I've worked across several industries as both employee and expert consultant in different parts of organisations. I've accumulated the necessary knowledge and experience to help business leaders adapt to this digital world from clients in Germany, Portugal and Saudi Arabia. These were businesses that needed my help, and their willingness to embrace and adopt my expertise has been inspiring. I hope that this book will inspire you in similar ways to adapt. I know that change is not always welcome, and it can be difficult to implement, but we can all learn from the lessons of Covid-19: wishing we had been better prepared masks the real issue that change (the digital era) was already happening. None of us can turn back the clock and avert the struggles ahead. While hindsight is a great thing, having the foresight to adapt to survive in the current climate is a gift worth its weight in gold.

Before you proceed any further with the book, you may want to take the opportunity to measure your potential to succeed as a digital leader. Don't be disheartened if your score is on the low side;

this book is designed to help raise your awareness as to how to be a successful leader that can compete and thrive in the digital era. Alternatively, the same scorecard will appear at the end of each chapter, the content of which may then prompt you to take the temperature of where you're currently at. (Note: in Chapter 6, the scorecard differs in that it measures your ability to build a successful digital product organisation.)

⊕ You can access the scorecard at: http://bit.ly/ Scorecard_ADAPT_Book

ONE

Approach

Whether it's a long-established business or a new enterprise about to set its course, for a business to survive and grow, it needs to have customers. In all probability, your own business has successfully traded for a number of years. It's enjoyed the fruits of a loyal customer base who purchased your goods and services either in-store, direct from your warehouse or from your online shop window. Your good name and reputation have consistently earned you excellent returns and dividends in the expectation that its profitability would continue for many more years to come. Until Covid-19 came along, that is. As I've explained in the introduction, this has proved to be a game changer in how we now need to continue to trade, resulting in a paradigm shift that will impact us all for many decades to come, if not permanently.

When the virus hit, tens of thousands of business owners were forced to physically distance themselves from their customers in person virtually overnight, making purchasing impossible or at best, a logistical nightmare. Unfortunately for many, the pandemic spelled the end of their enterprises altogether simply because their customer base no longer had access to their products. It would be easy to blame this economic disaster on the pandemic alone, and while that may be true for some, I contend that it's also a convenient explanation. The underlying reality is that in the digital age many traditionally run and struc-tured businesses had already failed to keep pace and adapt not only to the times, but to an ever-evolving set of customer behaviours. I'm not pointing the finger of blame at anybody or suggesting businesses have been reckless or stupid. Far from it – I understand that in a pre-Covid-19 world where certainty was more or less a given, it was easier to rely on a sense of complacency than it was to invest time, energy and resources into adapting a future-proof customer strategy. However, that sense of complacency was perhaps as equally catastrophic as the pandemic, and the battle for future viability and profitability was already at play before Covid-19 tipped the balance.

However pessimistic that may sound, there is a way forward that should give all executives hope, and it begins with how we approach the customer. Not only does the digital era drive sales – it also drives customer behaviour. Understanding that impact is vital. Business leaders need to recalibrate their approaches to retaining and acquiring new customers. These will necessarily be different to the accepted, traditional ways that are hangovers from the industrial era. My aim is to create greater awareness of how customer behaviours and expectations have changed – and continue to do so – so that we can pre-empt, react and respond to grab the attention of customers in the digital era. This is the only way that our businesses will survive and grow.

The digital era has revolutionised and disrupted how customers prefer to engage and purchase from businesses, with few exceptions. Many execs have found themselves running uphill in an ever-increasing, fast-paced race to meet the demands dictated by the changes in technology. The proliferation of smartphones offers customers the ability to connect to online store fronts and social media on a scale unimaginable at the turn of the century. Not only do customers actively engage with businesses, but they connect with each other – a key development in business reputation awareness and the impact of which I will outline in more detail below.

In the 'old days' (that I refer to as the industrial age), for the most part brands relied on mass market models which disseminated their offers to the entire marketplace without discrimination or post-analytic, detailed discernment. Basically, brands would hope to 'get lucky' that they would reach their intended customers as if they were casting bread on the water to catch a fish. In many respects that worked extremely well for brands that could afford a huge media spend, and those that could reaped the rewards. It was a time when big household brand names came to dominate the market, but it's important to reflect that the channels were limited, and so customers had little choice as to where they received their information from. Analogue campaigns such as advertising in high-circulation print titles or in expensive ad breaks during popular programmes delivered returns that justified the initial cost outlay. It was the golden age of binary broadcast marketing.

Today, that model no longer applies. Narrowcasting is the way to go, where 'narrow' is a misnomer in that it implies 'less'. The rise of the digital era is proving that, in fact, less is actually more. It's so powerful, it's attracted leading academic luminaries to carry out research studies on the topic. David L Rogers, a professor at Columbia University, has identified that the tables have turned. In his book, *The Network Is Your Customer: Five strategies to thrive in a digital age*,[1] his findings suggest that the marketplace is shifting towards a customer network model which in essence relies more on pull than push. Indicative customer behaviour shows that they are hungry for more than the simple 'buy, buy, buy' message of the traditional mass marketing model. Instead, they actively seek

---

1   DL Rogers, *The Network Is Your Customer: Five strategies to thrive in a digital age* (Yale University Press, 2003)

out content from the businesses they wish to purchase from in the form of websites, blogs, Twitter, social media posts and from other customers in a collectively shared experience (forums) that didn't exist on such a scale pre-twenty-first century. The mass market model no longer exists – it has been unapologetically usurped by the customer network model. The binary pattern of analogue communication ('we sell, you buy') is dead. The fact is, everyone is digitally connected: your customers are connected to your products and services, right through to your business core itself – from its stakeholders to its shareholders. Information is available to all, as is disinformation, and we can no longer expect our customers to behave in simple, compliant ways.

Customers aren't satisfied in responding to an advertisement and making a purchasing decision based on its message – they want to know more, they want to feel involved, aligned and valued in their purchases. The internet has changed everything. A new product released into the market can succeed or fail almost instantly thanks to customers seeking out and posting their own reviews. Is it good value? Is it a must have? How easy was it to purchase? How good (or bad) was the customer service? How many stars does it deserve? This behaviour is not confined to the big-name brands – it applies to *all* brands, thousands upon thousands of them competing for a share of their market niche.

Standing out in the crowd has never been more important. Never before has the customer been in possession of more knowledge about the product they wish to buy (other than perhaps the person trying to sell it). My message to any business leader struggling with this customer mind-shift or worried that their base might be diminishing is the good news that your customers are still there – they just need to be approached in a different way. While the customer network model does transfer the power to them, it also exponentially increases your opportunities to reach out to them when they come looking.

That's why I recommend anticipating, adapting your approach and then acting. Only then can you reverse any decline and see growth in your customer base. My business is based in Germany and Portugal, but my reach crosses the borders of Europe, the USA, Asia and the Middle East. That's because over the last few years I've diligently created digital assets that have reached beyond my operational base. Utilising available technology has enabled my business to penetrate markets where I was previously invisible. Broadcasting my message had never been within my power, but by harnessing the enormous power of the digital era and honing my focus, I have been able to broaden my reach by providing free valuable and educational content that then draws prospects towards my services I charge for.

My customers choose to interrupt their schedule to interact with me because this has become embedded purchasing behaviour. Mass marketing relies on a completely opposite approach where a business interrupts the customer without invitation to engage, running the risk of alienation or the message being ignored – especially if it's irrelevant. The pursuit of customers in the digital era has totally rewritten all the rules of advertising and the way we sell our products and services. If we are all to adopt the benefits of using the customer network model, we need to move away from mass marketing techniques. Customers are curious and savvy, they know what they want and they'll carry out their own research to inform their purchasing decisions.

It's in all our interests to actively be part of two-way conversations to help convert initial interest into sales. The rise in popularity of online chatbots and easier means of communication between vendor and customer increases the opportunities to drive sales. Engaged and satisfied customers then become your ambassadors and recommend your brand, products and services to family, friends and strangers. In financial terms, this marketing approach is a much better use of your financial resources, unlike the expensive mass market model in which you take a gamble in respect of actual conversions.

Investing more of your marketing budget in targeted, relevant and differentiated content will help drive traffic both directly and indirectly (eg via referrals) to your products. Engagement is key. It feels personal, and positioning your content and messaging within a context relevant to your industry greatly increases the chances of interaction and response. Use your content to educate customers about your product and select digital platforms and channels that most match your customers' browsing activity. Finding those points of shared value between you will inspire them. Earn their trust and listen to their feedback because that leads to further innovation and collaboration that can only benefit your future growth.

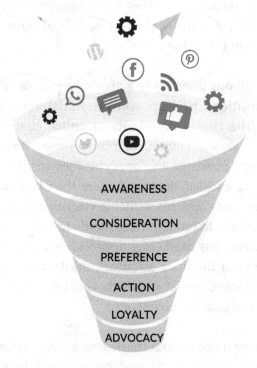

The sales funnel

Some executives remain sceptical or puzzled when I offer them this advice and still need some convincing that this is the route forward. I am occasionally asked if the traditional sales funnel is still valid. My response is, of course it's still valid, but it fulfils its function in a completely different way.

The typical sales funnel graphic shows what we would expect:

• Awareness

• Consideration

• Preference

• Action

• Loyalty

• Advocacy

While this sales funnel remains valid, its principles have been adapted to be more effective in the digital era. Whereas the traditional, mass market approach would rely on large numbers of potential customers receiving information via TV, radio, print media and physical promotional material and campaigns, the digital approach places the emphasis more on the niche customers' values and interests. Digital enables potential customers to find products and services more proactively via search engines, engaging with content and perhaps more importantly, via other customer testimonials. This aspect of customers acting as a brand or product's advocate via such an instantly searchable and viral medium is one of the most significant developments I can think of when knowing how to adapt in approaching, and attracting, your customers. When brands could control the messaging, it was the mass market approach that customers were influenced by, but in the digital era it is the customers themselves that can drive your product's message to reach others.

In today's context, loyalty and advocacy via social media are especially important elements of the sales funnel process and have turned it on its head. When a customer really likes a brand, they will actively seek out its social media channels to follow. This creates a two-way journey in which the brand needs to consciously nurture this relationship and show its loyalty towards the customer, repaying their interest by creating targeted, informative content that continually engages and inspires, leading to sales. With the rise of social media influencers, the ability to react and respond works both ways: a product released on one day can either be a hit or a miss by the next day. Listening to such feedback is a gift, and because it's instant, you must be on top of it at all times. It allows you to gauge the success of your product or where you need to improve. It needs to evolve into being a continual testing of the temperature of your relationship with your customers.

Five customer behaviours

In his book, David Rogers sets out five customer behaviours that businesses need to pay attention to when defining their digital approach:

1. They expect easy **access** to brands' products via their mobile or internet-enabled devices.

2. They want to **engage** in two-way communication with your content and services via apps, blogs and social media.

3. They expect **customisations** so that it feels personal and connects to their values.

4. They want to **connect** with other customers who hold similar values because it feeds their need to interact in a social context.

5. They want to **collaborate** with you to satisfy their desire to help create better products and services.

Access

In my own instance, enabling customers access to interact with my products and services maintains a stream of continuous two-way engagement. Informed by my own learning, experience and feedback from my customers, I assiduously create content (blogs, white papers, web content, PDFs for download) on a regular basis. When customers email me, I tailor my response so they feel that I'm paying due attention to their comments and questions. They welcome the opportunity to collaborate with me and they suggest ideas for improvement, which I welcome in return.

Engagement

Engaging with customers is a fundamental growth accelerator since it chimes with the direction of travel. It's not just today's customers that have modified their purchasing behaviour; it's the next generation of customers who have been brought up with these behaviours hardwired into their daily lives that need to be considered. They have grown up with ready access to technology and represent your sales, turn-over and profitability in the not-so-distant future. Today, it's second nature for teenagers, even children, to automatically grab their mobile devices to provide instant answers when they need information. Research carried out in 2019 by Common Sense Media showed that the average US teenager spent up to nine hours per day engaging with social media.[2] They know what they want, and how they want to achieve it. These are our customers, and they'll sustain the legacies of all businesses, so we must be extremely vigilant in recognising and adopting their behaviours

---

2   V Rideout, 'The common sense census: Media use by tweens and teens' (Common Sense Research, 2015), www.commonsensemedia. org/sites/default/files/uploads/research/census_researchreport. pdf, accessed 23 February 2021

now and incorporating these as essential business practice in how we structure our approach.

Many businesses are already riding this wave, such as Uber, with its targeted location recognition that tracks its users' behaviours and preferences no matter where they are in the world. Love or loathe Uber, it has its finger on the pulse, and where there's a pulse, there's life. Similarly, new car rental companies are disrupting the traditional service model of rent and collect from a fixed, often inconvenient, location, and now offer an app-based service which matches your position to the nearest available vehicle. Having located it close by, the smartphone app unlocks the vehicle and the customer drives away (some companies even drop vehicles off at a designated place). The result for the customer is minimal effort from reservation through to fulfilment.

This flexibility is a good indication of what customers are beginning to expect from the brands they engage with. As we dive deeper into digital, it will be up to individual companies how they take this behaviour into consideration to define which tailored approach best suits their offer to fulfil customers' needs and wants. It doesn't always need to a sophisticated fulfilment app – relatively simple techniques such as creating 'how to' videos online that demonstrate the power and effectiveness of your product can provide equally engaging customer experiences. Anything from how to tie your tent's knots, to baking a cake or replacing parts in an appliance – if the video expertly, clearly and easily explains what the customer is seeking answers to, they are more likely to follow through with a purchase via the link to your online store. Without this content available, your chances of visibility are much diminished and your approach to potential customers is unaligned, un-empathetic and distant.

Customisation

Customers no longer want to be regarded as a herd. Today, feeing and being treated as an individual has superseded the notion of a 'one size fits all' mentality, driven more recently by Millennials. This sensibility is also to a great degree because of the non-curated nature of the internet and it's 'on demand' capability. There are no all-powerful gatekeepers that decide what we choose to see, or when. It's a fluid landscape where there is something to appeal to everybody's taste. When a customer chooses to click on content, it's because it resonates as already being relevant to their interests and intellects. Get that content wrong and they'll soon abandon the site and migrate to another that satisfies them. That same niche capability is beginning to translate into how brands target their users via customisation. Uber, as I've already mentioned, has made great strides in harnessing this as a tool that speaks to the individual at a macro level. Its geolocation software recognises when its customer arrives in a new location and targets its offering accordingly based on its customer's behaviour. It's a small gesture but it can have a big impact on the customer who is not left feeling spammed by irrelevant marketing content. That experience can take the end user to a different level whereby they become more passionate about the brand. Similarly, if you subscribe to Netflix you might receive a watch-list recommendation different to that of your friend or neighbour. That's because Netflix employs software that analyses individual customer viewing habits and tastes so it can tailor its messaging accordingly. On a broader scale, when Coca-Cola introduced a comparatively low-tech, front-ended campaign which involved printing names on its bottle labels it proved to be a huge digital success, resulting in an uplift of sales by 7% among young adults after consumers began to share images of themselves and their 'personalised' bottle of Coke on social media.[3] The autosuggestion was that even a behemoth the size of Coca-Cola cared about its customers individually. It was no mean feat and is a fantastic example of being able to exploit a physical in-store purchase that managed to spread virally across the internet. It aptly demonstrates that customisation at any level of sophistication is a powerful sales driver.

Connect

Humans are pack animals and crave being social. The Covid-19 pandemic which saw millions of people

---

3   'Share a Coke campaign post-analysis', *Marketing* (22 June 2012), www.marketingmag.com.au/hubs-c/share-a-coke-campaign-post-analysis, accessed 29 March 2021

self-isolating for weeks on end went against our instinct to mingle with others. Thankfully, the digital world was still accessible by most in the confines of their isolation. The pandemic reinforced the notion that people seek digital experiences as a means of expressing themselves and to share their lives with one another. It underlined the need we all have, to feel connected with others.

Customers now know, if they didn't already, that they can survive without stepping outside their own front doors. In their relief following lockdown they may have flocked to coffee shops, bars and restaurants, but they will have retained a good measure of online reconditioning developed during circumstances imposed on them by decree. This will be difficult to shake off, so any business that fails to step up to the digital plate *will* eventually find itself at a disconnect between itself and its customers. If nothing else has convinced executives entrenched in the analogue, industrial age, the pandemic should certainly prompt them to think again when developing either their business or new products. The question that needs to be front of mind is, 'How can I enable my colleagues and my users to connect?'

This may sound daunting at first, but I know from my own experience that once I embraced it, it wasn't long before this became an essential tool in my digital strategy toolbox. I now relish opportunities to connect, with publishing online tips relevant to my business sector, or in creating content for online sign-ups for communities where my customers can attend an annual workshop for knowledge sharing and best practice advice. It's also an opportunity for me to listen, learn and grow.

Brands such as Dell already provide online portals where customers can feed back what new features they would like to see developed and introduced into the marketplace. SAP provides a community network populated with blogs and articles that encourage users to share, engage and collaborate with each other. Initiatives such as these can be as complex or as simple as best suits your business, but the principle of creating a service or a product where you can create a 'tribe' that allows your customers to connect with each other is essential.

Collaboration

As with socialising, people like to collaborate with one another. Collaboration helps us humans in our quest to find a common purpose. Look at Wikipedia – a collective, knowledge-sharing portal that spans the globe. Thousands upon thousands of people contribute their knowledge in the pursuit of fulfilling a bigger purpose without recompense. The same applies to drivers who use navigation apps especially enabled to report road accidents or incidents in real time so that they can pre-warn other drivers to change course and avoid delays. It's the same principle: thousands of strangers collaborating with each other in pursuit of the common good.

This philosophy is easily translatable to the business world: create and encourage your own community of strangers who will willingly connect because they have this innate desire to contribute to a bigger purpose. In your case, that will be helping you understand how you can make your product or service better than it already is. Many brands have wised up to this and created Facebook communities for customer support. In fact, this is more cost effective than traditional customer support functionality, since many of the problems raised by customers are resolved by the responses of others. Customers tend to trust other customers' experiences, and enabling transparent connection between them via the platform you create also tells them that you value and trust your connection with them.

Summary

The digital era impacts businesses of all sizes, from the multinational to the sole trader. When considering the digital transformation of your business, it's the customers and their evolving patterns of behaviour that need to be the centre of your immediate focus. Lose sight of that and they will lose sight of you. Preparation is vital – you need to align your products and services with new customer behaviours, and to create and build products and services that will connect your customers with your business and with each other.

It would be erroneous to believe that digital is synonymous with artificial intelligence or non-human interaction. Far from it – in fact, the opposite mindset is a more accurate reflection of the world that we operate and live in today. Circumstances have changed (and were already doing so pre-Covid-19 while we were all asleep), but so have customer behaviours. When once you might have reasonably expected to engage with your customer face-to-face, this is no longer the norm. Only by adopting a digital approach will businesses level the playing field and be able to compete for custom. In so doing, your business will engage with its customers on a more personal basis than it has ever done before. Not only will you get to know them and their needs in greater detail, they'll also learn more about you and what you stand for. Approaching your customers in the way I have described will lead you all to an increased sense of alignment. Once aligned, never forgotten.

In the Approach segment you have been prompted to consider how you currently attract customers and how well you educate them about your brand, products and services. If you didn't take the scorecard at the end of the Introduction, you might want to measure how successful you will be as a digital leader now:

http://bit.ly/Scorecard_ADAPT_Book

TWO

Data

For many executive leaders, data provides a snapshot about people, places and things in relation to operating their business. In its raw form data provides essential business intelligence extracted from a range of sources, from financial spreadsheets through to inventory. It can chart the ebb and flow of how well the business is performing and whether it's trading at a profit or a loss. In today's digital environment, data is more than an aggregated accounting exercise – it's a truly valuable commodity, more valuable than oil or gold. Understanding how you can deepen your relationship with data will greatly enhance your business intelligence. If you want to breathe new life into your company then data is one of the most important assets you have.

The problem is that for many small (and some surprisingly large) business enterprises that continue to operate using traditional, industrial-era practices, the value of data remains under-appreciated and under-resourced. The aim of this chapter is to reintroduce you to data to discover the myriad of capabilities that will help transform your business to make it a digital fit for the future. If you're possibly thinking that this is a task for your IT department or external consultant to handle, then I'd ask you to place that thought on hold for now. In fact, understanding and employing data will play to the strengths you already have as an executive leader – your strategical and operational planning capabilities. Data is a key business driver that you need to be leading with, guided by your data experts. Once you piece the data puzzle together you can effectively mine it and achieve deeper levels of intelligence so that you can leverage it. Data is key to understanding the success of your business operations and your customers' evolving behaviours. Unlocking your data opens the door to making more money.

Data, not dirt

I know that for many, when they hear the term 'data' it feels like the air has been sucked from their lungs. It leads to hearts sinking and eyes glazing over because, unless you are a natural statistician, it's not exciting. It's often overwhelming and can inundate a business with a single key stroke on the keyboard – 'submit'

– which is what many feel they must do: submit to large amounts of both structured and unstructured data. Like it or not, data pervades every business on a daily basis; because of that many leaders leave it to their IT professionals to pore over. However, it's not the amount of data that's important – it's what you do with it that matters. If it remains untreated, it's simply a mass of raw information and its only attraction is, 'How much have we sold today?' or, 'Are we making a profit?' This is extremely useful information, but it only skims the surface of what data can really do for a business.

All businesses inevitably collect data, although for many this is still an exercise in collation. Businesses that function in silos will invariably amass this data for individual departments such as HR, finance, sales and marketing, IT, stock control, etc. Therein lies the first problem with data – it's analysed purely along functional lines and ends up in separate silos, resulting in fragmented and fractured data. If it were to be analysed across the entire business then the performance in department A may well correlate to what data tells you from department B, etc.

Only when a business understands how to integrate *all* its data across *all* departments does it really begin to shine a light on the real health of the enterprise. Looking at data from a holistic viewpoint can tell executives how and where they can make better decisions to improve the overall health of the business, especially when impacted by events outside of their control.

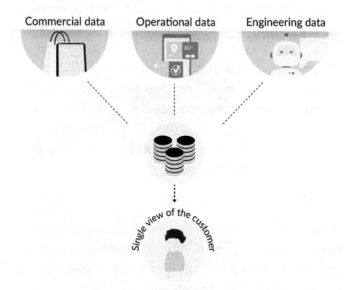

Commercial data   Operational data   Engineering data

Single view of the customer

Integrating different data types

Understanding this principle of cross-functional collaboration is central to the thesis of this book and in the following chapters I will outline how data acts as glue, so it's important to understand why I focus on it as a main pillar of the methodology. By the time you read the final pillar (Transformation) you'll understand why I hope to persuade you to shift any negative mindsets around data and instead embrace it as the valuable commodity it represents – something that can significantly extend your customer reach and increase your revenue.

Data helps you project and plan for future growth. For example, for a high street general store retailer (it doesn't have to be a large chain, it could be a family business), imagine the value of partnering with a mobile app weather forecasting provider. When the senior buyer or stock controller receives an alert of the long-term forecast that shows an extended period of rain, or a heatwave, appropriate levels of in-store stock can be ordered to meet the expected customer demand. Mobile apps are fast becoming popular within the car insurance sector where providers offer customers 'black box' capabilities which analyse driving data which is then used to set premiums at a tailored rate based on a customer's driving behaviour. Not only does this data often help reduce driver premiums (benefit to the customer) but it also helps the insurer to project the likelihood of pay-outs (benefit to the insurer). This is a classic example of using data intelligently to both improve customer retention as well as impacting on the businesses' financial health. Both examples show simple ways of combining data by combining cross-functional roles using data collecting apps. Data begins to prove its value to generate more money and value streams for customers when the business analyses it holistically.

Getting the best from your data

Not knowing how to get the best results from your data is not an excuse for not doing it. *You* don't need to be the expert – you simply need to be aware of its potential value. The first step in your data journey should involve engaging a partner to help you define your ongoing data strategy right across your business. (In Chapter 9 I will outline how to best source the right partners for you.) As you will rightly tell me, as an executive, you shouldn't need to worry about the IT complexities of data per se, because that's what specialists are for. I am not suggesting that you need to distract your attention away from your executive core responsibilities in delivering your company's vision, mission and values to generate revenue and profits. In today's world it's virtually impossible for you as a leader to know everything – and nor should you feel the need to. Your role is to appoint people into key internal positions or hire partners to help you form a 360-degree overview of what this book is offering you within the five pillars. Data is no less significant than any of the other pillars, and being aware of its potential and initiating a digital strategy is a good place to start. The first step will be to import data from different silos and departments to generate new insights into the whole business.

Case study: Metro

When I wrote my first book on organisational mastery,[4] I was consulting to a wholesale cash and

---

4   L Gonçalves, *Organisational Mastery: The product development blueprint for executive leaders* (Rethink Press, 2019)

carry company, Metro, in Germany. One of the data initiatives they implemented was using its data to analyse customer engagement from purchasing to retention. The objective was to accurately predict at which point customers would discontinue buying and move to another supplier. The data told them that we needed to trigger a front-ended action by appointing a relation support representative who would reach out to customers either thinking of switching to another brand, or to persuade former customers to return.

Customer acquisition is the most expensive element of the journey, after which your work is cut out in trying to retain them. In Metro's case, the business decided to invest in importing its data from across all of its departments. The reality was that predicting customer future behaviour was not solely confined to one – there were many trends from numerous departments that data could shed insights on. Combining that data offered a more complete understanding of how frequently, and how much money, customers spent, what the most popular products were, and how much it was costing the business to fulfil. As a result of this combined data analysis, Metro was able to build an informed and accurate picture to predict how engaged their customers were, and more importantly, how likely it was that they were looking to migrate.

Data equals dollars

Data is a valuable commodity – more expensive than oil. There are plenty of opportunities to sell it on to third parties where appropriate (I am not referring to selling customers' personal data, which is regulated by European GDPR legislation). When Nokia developed its own geo-location mapping service, it invested extensively in creating a detailed mapping service (Here.com – considered by many to be superior to Google Maps). The quality and reliability of this data product was recognised as a valuable acquisition asset by Daimler, Audi and BMW, who together formed a consortium to purchase Here Technologies from Nokia for $3bn in 2015,[5] beating rival bids from the likes of Uber. For the consortium, the acquisition was a move towards building their own platform for self-driving cars, which required precision mapping and GPS technology. For Nokia, offloading it cleared the way for the company's planned merger with Alcatel-Lucent. It was the lifeline the struggling Nokia brand needed as it had failed to keep pace with Apple's smartphone technology and its market share had rapidly declined. It was the data that it had accumulated that eventually became more valuable than its initial core proposition, which was the hardware.

---

5   T Connelly, 'Nokia agrees to sell its map service to German motoring giants for $3bn', *The Drum* (3 August 2015), www.thedrum.com/news/2015/08/03/nokia-agrees-sell-its-map-service-german-motoring-giants-3bn, accessed 29 March 2021

Its shareholders were saved because Nokia had the vision to create a data strategy.

As a business owner or executive, ask yourself the following questions relating to developing a data strategy:

- How will you create the data?

- How will you use the data?

- How can you then create value with that data?

To begin deconstructing this, there are three types of data you will need to incorporate into your strategic plan:

1. **Business process data:** This sits at the centre of your daily ops which are then managed, optimised, risk-assessed and reported on. It typically spans your inventory and supply chain, sales, invoicing and human resources.

2. **Product (or service) data:** This delivers the business core value proposition among others, eg, maps data (Waze, Google, HERE WeGo), business data (ZoomInfo, Bloomberg, Experian) and specialisms (AccuWeather, Epocrates).

3. **Customer data:** This provides insights into building a more complete customer base picture from purchasing and behavioural patterns, demographics and interactions.

Knowing those three key data types and then being able to cross-fertilise them across the business offers enormous, previously unseen, insights into your main focus, ie your customers' needs. For example, they can show you:

- Where they are

- What they want

- When they want it

- How and when you can deliver it

British Airways have nailed this with their data-fed, customer-led 'Know Me' programme. Its objective is to integrate data analytics from all the departments that customers interact with to shape its inflight customer service. They combine the data to form a single, detailed view of customers and their individual behaviours, tastes and preferences. This manifests itself in exceptional onboard personal customer service and extremely high levels of customer satisfaction:

Satisfaction + loyalty = $$$

Even with millions of passengers, the Know Me programme makes the customer feel recognised and valued. If your customer service provides this level of engagement to *everyone* that interacts with your brand, then it is differentiated from the competing brands that don't. No matter how big and unsexy it might seem at first, viewing data from the perspective of how your customers can benefit provides a different, powerful perspective.

Data can transform your business. *The New York Times* used to be a traditional print title stuck in the analogue age, but its owners knew that with the onset of digital media platforms and channels, it needed to compete on a level playing field.[6] They identified that using data would be the way forward to facilitating their entry into the digital era, but they also knew that their core business was creating editorial and printing papers. They brought in an external data expert to help them form their strategy – which was to become an essential pillar central to their business growth (it was non-existent until then). Using data, they literally changed the way they do business. Without bringing in the data expert, the paper's executive team would not have had any in-house knowledge of their customers. Installing data as a central pillar literally changed how the newspaper operated. It created an entire in-house IT department populated with data engineers whose focus was to test customers' subscription behaviours, discovering what advertisements converted into follow-through, what items most appealed to their interest and how they might then push these. Data also allowed them to optimise logistics in delivering the printed

---

6   H Tiersky, '*The New York Times* is winning at digital', *CIO* (8 June 2017), www.cio.com/article/3199604/the-new-york-times-is-winning-at-digital.html, accessed 31 March 2021

versions of the paper by analysing routes and traffic hotspots at peak times. Data allowed them to analyse orders and they streamlined accordingly based on accurately predicted demand, thus cutting costs while increasing efficiency. That's why I say that data is more valuable than oil.

What I'm *not* saying is that being digital means that you have a website. It's a mistake to believe that any business is 'innovative' simply because it has a web presence. That doesn't correlate at all. Prior to installing data as a core pillar of its business strategy *The New York Times* had a website, but it was simply another form of publishing its material without any forethought whatsoever. They didn't understand data, so they never collected it. As a result, they didn't know their readers. Selling newspapers in bulk to a street vendor or grocery store told them nothing about who their readers were – it was pretty much guesswork and fabrication based on circulation figures alone. That is not the same as having data. Had the newspaper owners not made the decision to enter the digital age with complete conviction by investing in its data pillar, the future of *The New York Times* may well have been cut short. Instead, it acknowledged that its traditional customer base (and, therefore, its advertising revenue) would dwindle if they couldn't find a means of offering customisation (such as subscription special deals), easy online access to quality journalism and more ways to interact. Data is therefore an inextricable extension of Pillar 1 of my methodology – Approach.

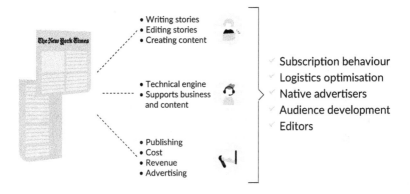

Data transformation of The New York Times

Big data

When George Orwell wrote his novel *1984*, he presented a scary vision of the future to a public not even used to watching television, let alone knowing what a mobile phone might be. His 'Big Brother' concept was perhaps a prefiguring of the big data yet to come. However intrusive and controlling that vision might have seemed at the time, big data *can* and *does* serve a purpose for the good of humanity. Big data is nothing more than unstructured data – it serves little or no purpose without proper interrogation. Structured data relies on:

- Advanced planning

- Organised presentation within spreadsheets or databases

- Qualified research drawn from inventories, surveys and tracking

Unstructured data is none of the above. In short, it's chaotic, kneejerk and unqualified, which serves no real purpose and offers no concrete insights whatsoever. It's to be avoided. Determining what unstructured data can tell us in respect of recognising patterns of behaviour or predicting trends has for a long time been problematic. Perhaps that's because, by its definition, this data was 'too big'? Analysts weren't sufficiently interested enough to deconstruct its enormous scale because they felt it couldn't really tell them anything useful. Until, that is, Covid-19 struck. That's when big data really came into its own. Mobile phone apps, using geo-location maps, were deployed on a mass scale (especially in Southeast Asia to begin with) to determine whether users had been in high risk of infection areas. It was a simple, but highly effective, way of putting big data to use with the end users' best interests at heart. Many thousands of gigabytes made up of unstructured data were mined from millions of smartphones and fed into the central monitoring servers to create patterns that had meaning and consequences.

When analysed contextually, unstructured data becomes a valuable commodity. There are three main components which each serve a different purpose:

1. **Social media:** Brands gain important insights from customer chatter, likes, dislikes, needs, wants, trends and what's falling out of favour. In the USA, movie exhibitors have been able to predict with notable precision which new releases are likely to sell well ahead of the first screenings and then increase capacity to meet expected demand.

2. **Mobile data:** Aside from the benefits gained from using mobile data during the Covid-19 pandemic, the same geo-location software is being increasingly employed by retailers to track trends in end users' movements that offer behavioural insights into what time of day they shop or eat in restaurants. Analysing this data builds up patterns of footfall, thus informing businesses when and where peaks and troughs in traffic occur. This is particularly useful in knowing when to roster staff.

3. **The internet of things:** With over fifty billion mobile devices in use across the world generating huge volumes of data, digitalisation is a key differentiator that enables companies to remain competitive. It enables businesses to collect and analyse data from connected assets, people and places to deliver actionable insights that can then lower costs, improve production quality, flexibility and efficiency and shorten response time to meet market demands.

Tools

There is no need for any executive leader to expend time, energy and personal effort in attempting to understand the technical minutiae of the tools that can help their business use the full power of data, but they do need to know that these tools are available to tackle unstructured data, and so are the experts to help implement a data strategy. If you feel that this all seems beyond your reach because you are a small business, I would have agreed with you only a few years ago. The reality is that all the tools you require are available inexpensively and are accessible no matter where you are located thanks to the proliferation of cloud computing services. You probably already make use of these services without realising it. For example, if you ask Alexa to choose your music playlist, request Siri to tell you the weather forecast, or open Google Maps on your phone, your commands are redirected to the cloud (unless you're offline). You no longer need megabucks to harness the power that the cloud offers, especially as your own hardware capacity isn't compromised in the process.

When Chinese technicians, working alongside oncologists, carried out a mass analysis of thousands of cancer patients' X-rays and analysed the resulting data, they developed a means of using AI to diagnose patients with a higher accuracy rate than by a human.[7] What this tells us is that, when diagnostically analysed, structured data in particular finds patterns that offer incredibly accurate insights into human behaviours that were previously inaccessible. AI technology increasingly provides huge quantities of big data that today saves us decades upon decades of undertaking painstaking development and research because this technology can also be applied across business sectors. In terms of the business world, big data might not foster any formal decision-making, but it's predicative capability will consequently inform better decision-making.

Value creation from data

As David Rogers correctly identifies, big data allows for faster, interconnected and informed business decision-making spanning four categories. These are as follows:

- Insights

- Targeting

- Value

- Personalisation

---

7   B Marr, 'Infervision: Using AI and deep learning to diagnose cancer' (Bernard Marr & Co, no date), www.bernardmarr.com/default. asp?contentID=1269, accessed 31 March 2021

Insights

Data reveals previously invisible insights into patterns of customer behaviours and preferences. For example, the Gaylord hotel chain in the USA identified the need to increase its number of customer recommendations as an objective. Their solution lay in text mining to understand the pattern of customer social media conversations. As a result of this analytical exercise, it became clear that from customers' reviews, likes and comments on social media, they valued the quality of their check-in experience more than any other aspect of the service they received. This insight informed the business that they should continually improve their check-in experience to generate more reviews that would promote increased traffic and awareness, and ultimately, reservations.

Targeting

In Pillar 1 (Approach), I was keen to emphasise the advantages of narrowcasting over broadcasting (mass market). What data analysis allows is a macro view of the target customer base in terms of identifying those customers most valuable to the business. Not all customers will be the same so there is little to be gleaned from data if they're hidden within a large pack. Targeting enables a closer examination of customer lifetimes, identifying repeat customers and those that remain loyal to the brand. It also shows different spend levels. A customer who purchases lower value products will be less likely to purchase higher value ones and purchase frequencies of customers may vary significantly to one another. It's pointless targeting customers with inappropriate offers measured solely against their spending behaviour. Once you analyse these patterns, creating a strategy for customers who habitually show that they are receptive to new products on a regular basis targets their known behaviours and is likely to result in a significant uplift in sales. This is especially important for customers that demonstrate repeated single-item, high-spend behaviours. Those customers then become the focus of more attention, with additional incentives to maintain that spending behaviour (the BA 'Know Me' model).

Personalisation

Data analysis enables the business to tailor its efforts to offer different, yet appropriate, experience for its users. A controversial example of this in action is when Cambridge Analytica embarked on a personalising data via Facebook across a large database of users based on a target demographic it was confident would be politically engaged by its messaging.[8] The principle behind it demonstrates how analysing data can unlock and customise an entire strategy, similar to

---

8   C Cadwalladr and E Graham-Harrison, 'Revealed: 50 million Facebook profiles harvested for Cambridge Analytica in major data breach', *The Guardian* (17 March 2018), www.theguardian.com/news/2018/mar/17/cambridge-analytica-facebook-influence-us-election, accessed 29 March 2021

when Coca-Cola identified that a significant portion of its customer base showed an interest in music.[9] This was then reflected in their advertising campaigns featuring musical artists enjoying a bottle of Coke while they played instruments or sang. On a subliminal level, this personalisation helped customers feel aligned to the messaging and product through adverts that matched their tastes.

Context

Context provides the reference in which the data relates to others. The most common examples that are in use are the large number of mobile phone apps associated with personal wellbeing and sporting activities. These track an individual's personal daily calorie intake, the breadth of their physical activity and their physiological response rates. While the customer gains personal insights into their daily lives, en masse the data gathered from these apps creates powerful behavioural insights brands can then use to provide valuable information to their customers.

Summary

In this chapter my aim has been to demonstrate the value streams that can be extracted from analysing

---

9   A Cook, 'Coca-Cola and music: A case study', *Music Business Journal* (May 2017), www.thembj.org/2017/05/coca-cola-and-music-a-case-study, accessed 29 March 2021

both structured and unstructured data. I specifically wanted to recalibrate our relationship with big data because the patterns it reveals offers us a far wider perspective of useful customer behaviour which can be harnessed in powerful ways, resulting in exponential revenue growth. As complex and obtuse as data in all its forms might at first appear, you should have now realised that as an executive, you don't need to be an expert in analysing or deconstructing this valuable information – it's enough to be aware of the potential that this data offers your business in ways previously unimaginable. Once you're able to implement a cohesive data strategy, you can then be the leader that takes your business to a completely different level. Love it or loathe it, data is one of the most crucial pillars for your business if it's to survive and thrive in the digital era.

In the Data segment you have been prompted to think about your current relationship with data and how you collect and then evaluate it to inform you about your customer trends and purchasing habits. If you haven't yet taken the scorecard, you might want to measure how successful you will be as a digital leader now:

⊕ http://bit.ly/Scorecard_ADAPT_Book

THREE

Agility

The Covid-19 pandemic was, without doubt, nothing short of an earthquake that took the world by surprise and shook businesses to their foundations. The stark reality is that for many it wasn't the virus and its deleterious effects that were entirely to blame for their demise – it was an entrenched mindset rooted in the industrial age that caused the walls of many a small (and large) business enterprise to crumble under the extreme pressure. Caught off guard and blinkered to the digital world around them, Covid-19 unashamedly accelerated the inevitable.

By adopting agility as a mainstay pillar, it's not too late to rebuild or to create from scratch a future-proof business that will be better prepared to thrive and survive in a world already feeling the seismic shocks of the digital era. In this chapter I outline how and why executive leaders must embrace agility as a mindset, and the advantages this offers. The mindset starts with you. Your agile leadership will enable your business to compete, survive and thrive in today's rapidly changing world and when the next global earthquake arrives, you will increase its chances of standing firm, in the same way that ductile seismic frames have saved many a skyscraper from collapse when the ground beneath them shifts violently.

Waterfall vs Agile approach

To gain agility, the shift in mindset I would like executives to make is a graduated migration away from the traditional Waterfall approach that many business visions were founded on during the pre-digital era towards Agile, an approach better suited to the digital age. Using the Waterfall model, a business begins the process of development with a perfect vision of the desired outcomes.[10] Agile, on the other hand, is intentionally blurred from the outset and leaves itself space and time to develop its vision.[11] Agile begins with an intent to achieve a goal, but it's not the perfect finished version – it's more blurred. Using an incremental (series of gradual steps) and iterative (making

10 'The ultimate guide... Waterfall model' (Project Manager, no date), www.projectmanager.com/waterfall-methodology, accessed 1 April 2021
11 'Agile 101' (Agile Alliance, no date), www.agilealliance.org/agile101, accessed 1 April 2021

progress through successive refinement) development process helps achieve the goal by knowing what's desired as an outcome within a landscape that is constantly shifting and evolving.

There is nothing inherently wrong with Waterfall, it's simply not an effective process to live by in the rapidly changing digital world. In business, the goal of Waterfall relies on setting that perfect image of the product/service from the beginning, and then investing inordinate amounts of time, effort and resources in achieving that. However, what happens when it's released into the market after such a lengthy development process but it's not up to par? Or when it is bested by a similar competitive product? It's tossed aside and discarded, and the investment is wasted. Not all the time, of course, but Waterfall naturally carries risk, which can be catastrophic. Waterfall works well in a non-complex process such as building a house, because that process is predictable. Imagine if Waterfall was applied to creating software, though – the designers and engineers would need to start from a point of complete certainty and perfect vision. It would be untested and unvalidated by the time it was released into the market or operations of a business. All the detailed planning from the outset might be worth nothing if the software is then deemed irrelevant and unworkable for its intended user base. Developing software is a different matter because, by its nature, it exists in a complex world in which execution does not always occur according to the plan. At any one point, a problem will occur that needs attention and requires adaptation. This complex world is one that most of us operate in these days, knowingly or not.

Applying Agile to software development allows the product designers to know they are heading towards a finished product, but creating it in stages allows them to push it out to the market. In this way they engage the customer (internal or external) in a conversation, asking them, 'What do you think? Because this is what we're thinking, and this is where we're at...' Agile invites incremental responses that speak to customer preference or answer customer need (even if they didn't know until that point that they needed it). Once tried and tested, the business can confidently claim it knows the lifecycle of that product, which in its final form can take on a life of its own.

Running a business for any leader *is* an extremely complex task in a world comprising thousands of ever-changing variables. The marketplace is one of continual evolution, which is why we need to consider introducing agility. Our mindset needs to change from setting annual goals because the market changes so rapidly. It's fine to know what direction the business is heading in, but goals should be broken into quarterly segments if it's to keep up with the pace of change. Agile demands a vision shift that leads to adapting, not just once, but always. The reality is, if your business still uses Waterfall as a process, it's completely surrounded by the Agile world around it and is hemmed in. That's why I urge all executive leaders to rethink it as a strategy, because Waterfall is no longer relevant in current society given that competitors are reading and responding to market conditions. Every business is its own complex world, and even if you've run a traditional business for many years, that success will, in all probability, be unsustainable in the near future, especially post Covid-19. Business leaders must accept a paradigm shift in thinking if they wish to remain relevant and no longer wish to struggle to survive.

Agile is agility in action

Agile is not a quick-fix process to dig a business from out of a hole. Please also do not be tempted to believe that Agile is simply a passing fad – it's not. Like the coronavirus, it will adapt and mutate to suit its future hosts. Nor is it a uniquely twenty-first century concept – even during the industrial revolution itself, the more successful business giants of the time recognised the need for agility and embraced aspects of Agile methodology. Think of the mill and factory owners who knew that generating steam, and then electricity, would be game changers in terms of their productivity and profitability. They adapted their operations by relocating their premises close to running water sources that powered their steam turbines and installed coal-fired engines that drove up productivity. That was agility in action – reacting and responding to technology that would exponentially increase their success and market share. The digital era is no different, except that today the rapid, eye-watering pace of change can outrun the best of us if we allow it. No business can afford to remain complacent, especially because they can't afford to develop ideas and products over lengthy periods (by that, I mean over months and months) and without refreshing their products and service offerings on a regular basis. If nothing else, Covid-19 will have prompted many to recognise that they need to adapt – now.

Times have changed and we are no longer bound by the perfect Waterfall visions that suited the industrial age. The digital-age-savvy business leaders that understand the power of agility thrive in a landscape filled with opportunities that they're eager and willing to exploit to their maximum potential. Agility is not simply a fancy word steeped in business philosophy; it's that mindset I referred to which sets them apart.

Of course, quite possibly you are already familiar with the term Agile in the business sense but haven't yet given it much consideration beyond being a buzz-word that has little, or no relevance to your business practice. If you have adopted Agile, you still may not have reaped its reward or fully understood its full potential, especially if it was introduced as a tick-box exercise to enhance 'training'. In that respect, it's often viewed as a badge of excellence, but if it's not fully embedded as an *ongoing* process that is continually reviewed, refreshed and redrawn at regular intervals, it never has the opportunity to shine right across the whole business. This is the main reason why I want executive leaders to understand that agility, and adopting Agile, is a mindset that begins with them. It's not simply a process that should be delegated to a consultant expert for the IT department. Agility is a *state of mind* and it must be executive led. Agile then works best when it's applied cross-functionally, not just at team level. Left within a departmental silo (as often is the case), eventually it will suffocate. However, when a leader understands the benefits that agility delivers, Agile has the potential to accelerate value delivery. Agility also maximises opportunities for the business to react and respond quickly, such as when Facebook (no stranger to agility) increased its capacity to provide video calling features during the Covid-19 pandemic to compete with Zoom's conferencing product. Facebook consequently adapted and added several new video calling features to its subsidiary brands of WhatsApp and Messenger as well as to its main app, following increased demand for social video calling, temporarily sending the Zoom share price tumbling.

Agile accelerates value delivery

From a cash flow point of view, Agile creates a stream of value delivery and enables money to flow faster. Compared to Waterfall, Agile accelerates value delivery. For example, with software development, it's possible to incrementally release 5% of the intended final product within as little as three months from its startup development into the marketplace, yet it's still 100% usable. Of course, there may not be the same full functionality that it will eventually have twelve months down the line, but by releasing it into the market sooner at a lower introductory price, it's possible to begin generating revenue and customer feedback. This can have a huge impact on improved cash flow, compared to Waterfall and its requirement for up to one year of full salaries. Agile only depends on funding two or three months of salaries up front, after which the business can incrementally charge more and more for its product.

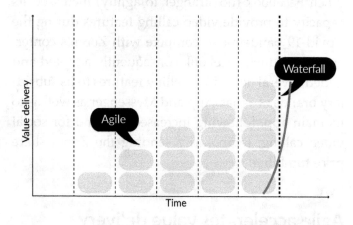

Early value

I am happy to repeat myself when I say the journey towards agility begins with you, the leader, so that you act as the example that everyone involved in the business can then follow. If you're not the one executing your own ideas that will send out a clear message that the strategy lacks real substance, and that agility is little more than a slogan. The most successful companies that I've seen are those that have inspiring leaders that totally commit to what they tell their colleagues as well as overhauling practices associated with the industrial era. That requires a more holistic approach, which breaks down inter-departmental rivalries and instead fosters collaboration between them. The outcome is that this shift in mindset leads to creating an organisation that focuses on products and services where the customer is placed at the centre of *everything*. Your leadership in this respect is what will connect your vision with overall strategy, enabling your business to incrementally adapt, grow and to become more competitive and cutting-edge in its mission to serve your customers. The result will be a business enabled to deliver better and be fit for purpose.

Risk reduction

You may be concerned that adopting a huge paradigm shift in both your thinking and practice carries a risk. In one sense that's true because people generally do not like change, it can make them feel uncertain or anxious. The greater risk, however, is making no change whatsoever while the digital era continues to evolve around you, because, as described in the previous chapter, your customers' behaviour is also evolving. The changes you implement across your whole business are a series of small but powerful steps in a fast and ultra-responsive manner, so the risk level is significantly reduced (as explained when comparing the Waterfall vs Agile models above). Instead of developing a product over a lengthy period at huge expense, you eliminate the risk of creating one that is unsuitable or disliked by your customers.

Bear in mind that your 'customer' may also be an internal person who will consume the output and is looking to gain value from what it produced. 'Customer' feedback and validation is, therefore, vital in the developmental processes since it allows immediate interaction, which can be followed through by incrementally improving the product. Risk is reduced and more manageable as a result and your investment is protected going forward.

As an executive leader reading this book, your business might feel incredibly at risk when the economic climate changes around you through no fault of your own, especially if your business success is predicated on an industrial-age model. After reading this book in its entirety I hope you will realise that agility is key to mitigating against that sense of risk which you're perhaps fearful of. The temptation might be to believe that yours is an irrelevant enterprise, but I would urge you to reconnect with your original vision, mission and values that have for so long served your customers.

Control variance with planning cadence

As described above, using the Waterfall model in any product development process risks the resultant 'perfect' vision being less than perfect by the time it's released into the marketplace. The lack of iterative planning, incremental testing and feedback that then informs the next iteration, as well as simply being behind the curve in a rapidly changing world, can render the product unsuitable and irrelevant, with little opportunity to achieve minimal ROI. In the digital era, ignoring those variations in the planning process, will seriously undermine the efficacy and viability of the business.

The Agile model, however, helps control these variations by implementing the cadence of planning. Rather than delivering the 'perfect' vision in the form of a complete product at the end of the process, planning involves adapting the product by running regularly scheduled sprints (set periods of time during which specific work must be completed and made ready for review) if not every two weeks, then at least each month, without fail. The purpose behind this approach is so that the product developers can review and measure each iteration against customers' needs and expectations.

Both customers' needs and expectations will always shift throughout any product development phase, so it is far better to gauge these regularly. Based on the feedback and validation following each synchronised sprint and product release, the developers can further adapt and re-adjust the product with incremental improvements until the blurred vision becomes perfect. Once again, bear in mind that the 'customer' may be internal to the organisation or be the end user who makes a purchase from the business. This typifies the cadence in planning that energises the developers and all the product team members involved (which I describe in the following chapter). Cadence planning controls these variations, and the payoff is that the business isn't left with a product that nobody really wants (therefore reducing risk while increasing customer validation). It enables maximum flexibility, which in turn is facilitated by maximum fluidity in which everyone involved is fully engaged, motivated and inspired *on a daily basis.*

In comparison, the Waterfall process funnels employees into a pressure chamber experience as its front-ended construct squeezes effort, time and energy into punishing crash and burn deadlines. Of course, deadlines are essential, but with the Agile approach they are graduated into a series of more manageable mini deadlines over the duration of the development process, at the end of which the developers have adapted and re-adjusted the product having taken into account customer feedback and validation.

How to apply the Agility model

Let me be clear: if the leaders and executive team of an organisation do not apply the Agile model themselves, the whole process will not work. Applying this method is not a process or task that should be delegated or limited to product teams and their management. It requires cultural and operational change that permeates the whole organisation. Failure to make this change will only extenuate any existing disconnects, and within a matter of time the organisation will fatally malfunction. This may seem like an exaggeration on my part, but I have witnessed this happen in a number of organisations.

For leaders to successfully introduce the Agile model in their organisations, the starting point on the roadmap therefore begins with themselves. As with undertaking any significant long journey, being prepared for what lies ahead is essential.

Awareness

As a leader, having awareness of Agile methodology is key to its successful implementation. I recommend that leaders and the executive team set aside the necessary time to meet offsite with a reputable and specialist consultant so that over the course of two days they can begin to clearly understand what Agile represents: how it impacts on the organisation, and how the executive leaderships' own work will also change as a result of its implementation.

Training

When the leadership have increased and absorbed the importance of awareness, they need to facilitate training for middle management. The leaders' objective here is to enable its middle management core to be trained to become exemplary coaches and leaders that can implement Agile effectively and inspirationally across the operational workforce. This is then followed by training the actual product teams themselves, where the focus is aimed at the implementation practicalities and frameworks such as Scrum, Kanban, etc (phrases you will become more familiar with, and appreciate the importance of, as you increase your awareness of Agile).

Implementation

Since this is key and pivotal to the whole future success of the organisation, my advice is – do not go it alone. To ensure that the implementation of Agile runs as smoothly and as effectively as it can for your organisation, bring in an external expert to help for the initial six months.

As a leader, when you consider introducing Agile teams into your organisation, don't make the mistake of believing it's a simple quick fix that can be resolved by a couple of days spent on a training programme. Committing to Agile ties into the long-term strategy and vision of the business which will create significant cultural changes in your business. It requires investment, both intellectually and financially, because this will be the catalyst for your business to change, pivot and then grow in the digital environment. If your intention is to stand out as a successful leader in the digital marketplace it's vital that you understand the three key steps outlined above: awareness, training and implementation.

Failure to follow these three basic steps will lead to a failure of proper implementation and the business will ultimately suffer as the result of a disconnect between the executive leadership (because it doesn't implement Agile), middle management and the product teams working on the front line. If you want your organisation to change, then you must change too. Leaders cannot create the organisation's Agile strategy if they're not prepared to apply Agile to the way they work themselves and be fully involved with its implementation. Agile is a significant financial investment in change, so it doesn't make sense for the leadership to continue carrying out its responsibilities without changing themselves. A fixed mindset is a major contributing factor in 90% of Agile implementations ultimately failing because the executive leadership failed to be involved in the transformation that Agile offered. The result is catastrophic, from the wasted investment spent on training management through to mounting levels of operational frustration which leads to stress and burnout on all levels. Each time the organisation tries to make adjustments, the failure of the leadership to be involved in Agile only serves to heighten the discrepancies and structural faults within the organisation. After several attempts, nobody in the organisation buys into Agile. Any plans the leadership then had for potential growth and success will most likely fail.

Summary

It's clear that in today's rapidly changing world, standing still isn't viable as a strategy. Each week the business landscape changes, sometimes in a nuanced way, at other times more dramatically (as with the Covid-19 pandemic). No business can afford to operate under the guise of the industrial-era model when it's the digital age that's in the driving seat. The digital age has long been the threat hiding in plain sight, but it was the Covid-19 pandemic that precipitated the need for traditional businesses to adapt and change at speed so that they can sustain growth and compete on a level playing field. This chapter has introduced agility as an asset that executive leaders must embrace for themselves to be the example that inspires and facilities change within their organisation if it is to meet the challenges posed by the digital age. Adopting Agile methodology, as opposed to Waterfall methodology, expedites change incrementally, but quickly, by which your business can measure real results in reducing risk, value delivery and by controlling variance through cadence planning. This needs total commitment to implement change in the full understanding that agility is not a process – it's a state of mind. It's also the only solution if a business wants to continue fulfilling its vision, mission and values in its bid to serve its customers in the digital age.

✔▬ In the Agility segment you will be prompted
✔▬ to reflect on how effectively your organisation
●▬ implements Agile (if at all), including at executive leadership level. If you haven't yet taken the scorecard, you might want to measure how successful you will be as a digital leader now:

🌐 http://bit.ly/Scorecard_ADAPT_Book

FOUR

Product

Applying Agile methodology to product requires executive leaders to rethink how they formulate their product development strategies. It requires a paradigm shift away from the single-focused approach of creating projects, towards organising strategies centred around products.

In this chapter I will explain how that shift in focus away from project to product creates a product life-cycle that is totally reliant on iterative discovery. Firstly, I will describe some of the barriers that executives of traditional companies have that prevent them from considering changing their mindset. No matter what business you run or what product or service you provide, my aim is to get you to think about product in an entirely different way by the time you reach the end of this chapter. Recalibrating your thinking about, and relationship to, product, and learning how to adapt it iteratively via incremental release into the market, will help you and your executive colleagues find these answers about your product: its desirability, feasibility and viability. This is not just woo-woo terminology. It's highly relevant in today's digital era, and by including it as a significant part of your strategy it will also save you money. The term re-evaluation is central to my argument and I will explain how this greatly enhances the way your product – and therefore your business – relates to its customers.

My principal frustration is executive leaders' firmly held belief that if they invest in a product, there will be a demand for it that will repay and reward that investment before it's even been tested or validated by customers. Executives need to think of product in an entirely different way – one that prevents spending so many resources and instead dedicates their efforts towards innovation and managing a portfolio of products that embrace agility. Unless your business is the same scope and size of an Amazon or a Google, it won't have millions in the bank that affords it to invest in products with an increased risk of failure when released into the market. Instead, use that money wisely, especially if yours is a business startup where cash is limited. In adopting agility as a central pillar of your organisation, that lack of cash is actually a huge advantage in evaluating your investment versus risk at every step. That's the same mentality I advise organisations of *all* sizes to adopt. The worst that can happen to a small- or medium-sized business with this mindset is not failure. Understanding why failure occurs invests the executive leader with great power because continually gathering the data via evaluation and discovery is worth its weight in gold. Of course, many executives would argue that they don't invest without some form of evaluation, but my argument is that agility is the key driver to achieving the desired outcomes that these questions seek to answer:

- What's the big idea you want to achieve?

- What's your strategy?

- Is this market big enough for your product?

Within the ADAPT Methodology® framework, these questions can save millions that could be spent on innovating a robust, relevant and tested product portfolio that the market needs (or anticipating its needs) and will help the business survive, especially when conditions are tough. Agility provides the tools to rethink your product portfolio with the maximum of flexibility, from strategy to delivery. The big difference is that it enables *discovery* that giants such as Facebook, Google and Amazon excel at. The problem for many businesses, including traditional ones (eg in the banking and insurance sectors), is what happens before delivery? How do they decide what to deliver, when and what cost? These are decisions already connected to the business strategy, but they tend to be geared towards thinking in terms of *projects* and not *product*. This is the mindset that needs to shift so that the thinking becomes more focused on:

- What products does the business intend to deliver?

- How can the business better deliver those products?

Understanding the concept of the value of information is vital, but without agility, executives make decisions too soon and they can be often the wrong ones. That's because a particular new initiative for a product is viewed from the wrong end of the lens as a project to be completed and where the outcome is the focus, as opposed to the iterative journey that takes them there incrementally (as described in the previous chapter). The paradigm shift from project to product needs to be part of every executive's thinking for all the reasons I have already mentioned.

This begins in understanding that Agility and Product work hand in hand. At the beginning of any endeavour (eg a new product, an enhancement to an existing product, or an exciting discovery from the research and development department) there are typically levels of uncertainty in the three key product areas:

1. **Desirability:** Will it sell?

2. **Feasibility:** Can it be built? (Is there a positive business model? Does it need partners? Does the business have access to the markets through the right channels?)

3. **Viability:** Will it make money? If so, how quickly and what's the ROI?

My advice is to take your attention away from the desired outcome and focus on the beginning.

The value of information

At this point, the curve of uncertainty is high. As the following diagram shows, your uncertainty can be significantly reduced even through minimal information gathering (and you can also substitute 'information' here with 'investment').

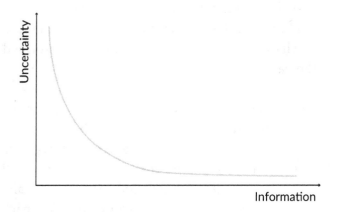

The value of information

The more information is gathered, the more investment is required to reach the next level of information. The next chunk of information might answer whether the business model is viable, or if the market is big enough to sustain this business model and what or where the customer pain points are along that curve. However, the value of information isn't tied into simply knowing how much profit will be generated if all the conditions are right to proceed – it's also about the sizing of the teams that will deliver it from day one. That doesn't mean deploying a full-size team of fully-fledged developers immediately at the point the when the business is evaluating the market opportunity. Instead, it may initially only require a small team of experts, such as a market specialist or researcher and a product manager. As more information is gathered and evaluated, you can then gradually involve specific engineers and designers should the product require a prototype. This iterative approach reduces uncertainty and risk until such point that the initiative is close to crossing its red lines or is looking viable enough to commit to fully. All the while you are making progress informed by the value of the information.

The more the product evolves, the more customers can be included by inviting their feedback through interviews or surveys or by trying out prototypes as they are released. The more you learn, the more you'll get close to what the market needs and can sustain. Further along, taking into account the feedback received, you can begin to test the market more fully by developing and releasing a minimum viable product (MVP):

- Minimum – it's not fully developed.

- Viable – you are validating the business model.

- Product – it's an actual, workable product, not a test.

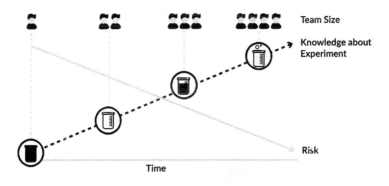

Growing the team

Some executives shy away from MVPs as part of product development, but I see them as essential in that they begin to evaluate actual functionality, usability and desirability, potentially avoiding wasting further investment should it fail. One of the most common misconceptions is the belief that the MVP is a test. Assuming that an MVP determines that its viability is agreed, ie it's functional, usable and offers value that customers will accept, then it can evolve further, and at this point you should increase the product team. If that product is technologically or scientifically based (eg a software-based or pharma product), the biggest risk will be a technical one. Agile allows the development team and the business to evaluate risks incrementally and iteratively. Only this approach offers more flexibility in managing invest-ment. That may either be knowing that the problem cannot be solved internally, engaging an external and willing partner to collaborate, or, in the worst-case scenario, to call a halt to its development altogether. In the latter instance, having ring-fenced the investment, the remaining budget can be allocated elsewhere. Operating under the traditional Waterfall model, the total budget would usually be spent by the time the product is killed, having failed to iteratively create a prototype, solicit market feedback and then create an MVP version.

This is why I emphasise that Product adopt Agile methodology founded on a product mindset versus a project mindset, which is often victim to 'the urgency paradox'. I'm sure that many executives will be familiar with this scenario, whereby a team concentrates its entire efforts over many months until it reaches a critical point in its progress when *every-thing* is suddenly urgent. Development teams then find themselves under increased and undue pressure to meet the designated release deadline and dozens of people are frantic to deliver the entire project as promised to the market. The fallacy of this approach is that the development period itself is when the cost of opportunity is spent in direct correlation to the expected ROI. We need to think about product not as a final outcome but as the result of an iterative journey. The difference in approach is demonstrated by the figures below.

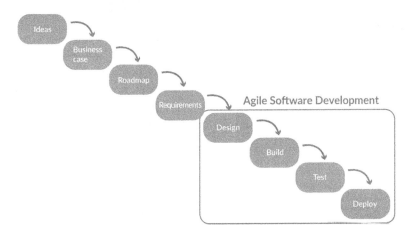

Project mindset

When Product is viewed as a state of mind, it also changes behaviours – the biggest change being the combination of discovery with delivery instead of focusing predominantly on the delivery alone. It's a more holistic approach that absorbs the natural ebb and flow in any startup or product development. The beginning involves a deep dive over several weeks into discovery, after which it's possible to begin a level of delivery (which also forms part of ongoing discovery).

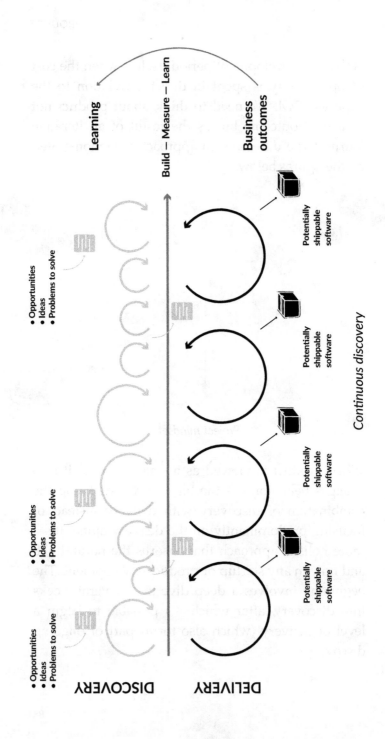

- Opportunities
- Ideas
- Problems to solve

- Opportunities
- Ideas
- Problems to solve

- Opportunities
- Ideas
- Problems to solve

DISCOVERY

DELIVERY

Learning

Build — Measure — Learn

Business outcomes

Potentially shippable software

Potentially shippable software

Potentially shippable software

Potentially shippable software

Continuous discovery

This new thinking means that every product team should be viewed as a value stream and should behave as if it were a startup, continuously scanning the market and trends while continuously trying to evolve its business model by using discovery as its foundation. It also means that your product solves the problems your customers are trying to solve, not what you're currently delivering. The focus must always be directed towards delivering customer value, and this is also continuous. It's fluid, not fixed.

This is what real business agility feels and looks like. It provides executive leaders the capability to change direction quickly due to constant evaluating in a 360-degree way from the strategy and the products through to delivery. It drives forward the business with perpetual motion, whereby discovery and delivery work in tandem, gathering market intelligence and knowledge along the way. Significantly, you learn more about what the customer wants, whereas in the project mindset, while you feel like you're moving forward, what you're actually doing is trying to reach a fixed point of arrival. In that case, when you do arrive (at the Waterfall's edge), the only remaining action is to jump until you hit the ground. If you're lucky, you might keep running; more often, it will be a dead drop to the bottom resulting in failure – that most dreaded of outcomes by many executives. A continuous mindset in place from the beginning *allows* you to fail, but to fail fast and then learn without losing momentum.

It may sound counterintuitive to welcome failure because, traditionally, failure is not an option. In my experience, up to 80% of business ideas will fail (and at great expense), but we should be thinking of failure as integral to the ROI. In basic terms, it's the difference between spending ten million on developing a product under Waterfall and it failing upon release, and spending one million through Agile and then pulling the product because discovery and data informs you it won't fly. This leaves nine million remaining for further product development in the same way that venture capital works. At the start of any new product development or business idea, you can be confident that you are buying answers to the questions raised above and that the answers are intrinsically linked to the problems your customers are trying to solve.

For example, when Nokia released a road traffic monitoring system in 2004, it was predicated on the basis that the business was known for producing hardware (handsets). The product it created was also rooted in a hardware solution in the form of static hardware boxes that were installed along roadsides. It sounds useful, but in fact, there was little customer application that appealed. At the same time, a small entrepreneurial startup based in Israel called Waze created a similar traffic monitoring product, except it was designed as an app that could be installed on a mobile phone. The key difference was that it put the customer experience at the heart of the product, because it allowed drivers who used the app to send and receive real-time information on traffic conditions. It was incredibly successful; so much so that Google acquired the business.

The error that Nokia made was the belief that their products were solely based in hardware devices, as opposed to understanding that their product was all about helping people. Whereas Waze came to understand through discovery and innovation that customers' behaviour was shifting towards mobility and the ability to interact. They listened to their customers' pain points and adapted their product to meet their needs, even though this was relatively new technology at the time and customers were still coming to terms with advances in mobile applications. Its success lay in discovery and that was a key element of the product lifecycle once feasibility and viability had been established. The magic happens when you know the 'how much' and the 'why'. This explains the need to include data scientists and data analysts in your product teams. If you were tempted to skip Chapter 2 on data because you were unsure whether it would apply to your business, I urge you to read it.

Summary

For me, a product is something that has life until it dies. It can live for anything from just one year or span a quarter of a century or more. The notion that a product has life should inspire and excite us all, because it implies continual evolution. To survive, products need to evolve, because the market and the channels where they're visible are also continually evolving. Who knows what the next TikTok, Instagram or Facebook will be? One thing for certain is that new channels and platforms will appear at regular intervals, each with their own demographic base and penetration. There is no longer such a thing as a zero-sum game when it comes to product. Keeping products alive in the digital era is of paramount importance if they are to be relevant to old, new and future customers.

From an organisational perspective, that same sense of life engages and inspires the people working within it. The project mindset is beset with numerous barriers and impediments. Ultimately, projects die – usually after that innocuous spell of trying to squeeze blood, sweat and tears into the entirely unnecessary 'urgency paradox'. With the emphasis turned towards the product, its iterative lifecycle and incremental improvement keeps it growing. It has a vitality that doesn't accept failure as defeat or the end of the road. For the people working on the product, they'll not experience the steep, often highly pressurised climb only to fall over the edge of the waterfall. Instead, they'll be more likely to continue in their employment, they'll be inspired by each new discovery. This will in turn engage and energise, which is vital in the need to innovate. When they're focused on a product and not a project, they are aligned to what the company is building.

✔▬
✔▬ In the Product segment you will be prompted
●▬ to think about your products' MVP and if they both inspire your customers and anticipate their future needs. If you haven't yet taken the scorecard, you might want to measure how successful you will be as a digital leader now:

⊕ http://bit.ly/Scorecard_ADAPT_Book

FIVE

Transformation

I began this book based on the assumption that you've been concerned by the rise of digital competitors in your business sector, which has resulted in a graduated fall in customers and revenue. Where once they walked through your doors in large numbers, called your hotline to place an order, or yes, even visited your website, those numbers have steadily declined. The Covid-19 pandemic has only exacerbated this – especially knowing that the world may yet have to live with such events more frequently in the future.

At this fifth and final pillar of my ADAPT Methodology,® I hope that I've persuaded you enough to consider making some important shifts in your business thinking and to recognise that it's not simply catastrophic global events that threaten your liveli-hood. The reality is that, for many traditional compa-nies, the headlong march of the digital age poses the greater risk to your business survival; because it's here to stay and its reach will inevitably increase. Like a life-threatening virus, it's been spreading unseen by those unaware of its true impact for years. Unlike a pandemic, however, it's a powerful force for good. My message of hope is that we each hold the power to harness its momentum. Once we understand how to apply its power more effectively, we can all achieve great things for our businesses long into the future.

The previous four pillars explain the need to imple-ment processes that will improve customer-focused outcomes, but this chapter is not just about the need to adapt – it's about creating transformation across the entire business, so this might seem the most difficult step to manage at first. I want us to delve deeper into the heart of the organisation itself, into areas where transformation is most needed to reshape it for the digital era. With that in mind, I've identified five key areas:

- Translating strategy into operations

- Reducing time to market

- Continuous improvement

- Knowledge sharing

- Innovation

These are the essential elements of my organisational mastery blueprint described at length in my book of the same title.[12] I will outline the headline principle of each in this chapter because this pillar is the glue that binds the rest together and helps translate state of mind into action. It also serves as a reminder that over the last 100 years, society has changed and the world is no longer as static as it once was – it's a fast-paced, changing environment that we all need to constantly adapt to and evolve with. In the early twentieth century, it was OK for Ford to offer its customers cars in any colour of their choosing, as long as that colour was black. That's not OK for customers today – they are much more demanding. Of course, Ford remains a strong and competitive brand and has made its own adaptations over its lifecycle.

Change is necessary for all businesses. While a company established in the 1970s might have expected to last for seventy-three years, today, a new company might be lucky to reach its twelfth anniversary. According to Professor Richard Foster from Yale University, the average lifespan of a company listed in the S&P 500 index of leading US companies has decreased by more than fifty years in the last century – from sixty-seven years in the 1920s to just fifteen years by 2020.[13]

---

12 L Gonçalves, *Organisational Mastery: The product development blueprint for executive leaders* (Rethink Press, 2019)
13 K Gittleson, 'Can a company live forever?', BBC News (19 January 2012), www.bbc.co.uk/news/business-16611040, accessed 30 March 2021

If companies fail to adapt at their core, then sadly, many will die. This includes startups. I'm often surprised that so many startups today believe they're modern and fit for the digital age when, in fact, their organisational structures are founded on building blocks laid down 100 years ago. I see functional departments time and again that, despite adopting Agile, remain project-led and confined in silos, thus creating impediments to growth. My aim is to show you how to transform your business into a modern organisation optimised for the digital era. You can do this by understanding and then incorporating the ideas I've expressed in the first four pillars that sit within the framework I am about to describe.

Organisational mastery

Over the years I've worked with many executives and managers to help them transform their organisations. As a result, I've identified several challenges that are common across all organisations. These include:

- Difficulties in connecting company strategies to everyday operations

- A heavy workload but nothing meaningful is delivered in the process

- Barriers that prevent scaling and enhancing the business

- Lack of innovation

- Recruiting and retaining the best talent

For many, old habits and traditions die hard, and unfortunately this is reflected in the mindset and skills of the senior management. This remains the greatest obstacle organisations hoping to compete in the digital era face today. Below, I explain how and why, it's crucial to help organisations restructure their day-to-day operations to guarantee they always prioritise their most impactful, revenue-generating products or services.

Translating strategy to ops and portfolio management

In Pillar 3, I write about the need for organisations to be agile to respond quickly to feedback and market conditions. Linked to this is the organisation's ability to connect and translate strategy into daily operations. This requires total clarity on where you want the company to be within the next five years. When I introduce this to my client, I usually work with practices such as Agile portfolio management or objectives and key results (OKRs), in which ideas, vision or objectives are generated.

1. **Agile portfolio management:** A process that deals with how an organisation identifies, prioritises,

organises and manages different products. This is done in a streamlined way to optimise the development of value in a manner that's sustainable in the long run.

2. **OKRs:** A process where the goal is for every member of the organisation, from the key stakeholders and leaders to all team members, to understand the objectives of the company through a set of defined, specific and measurable actions (for a more detailed description of OKRs, please refer to my book *Organisational Mastery*).[14]

These are then broken into annual objectives, following which I recommend establishing a cadence of quarterly reviews where executive leaders and their teams meet to identify four or five strategic goals they want to achieve. They are then disseminated throughout the whole organisation and need to be connected to one-year goals *and* to a five-year strategy. The flexibility this offers is vitally important when situations change. For example, just as Covid-19 swept across the globe, one of my financial clients (an online banking portal) was immediately able to switch from offering its popular customer-focused, travel-related service (Forex, travel affiliate services and destination guides) to helping parents have a better experience while they were at home in lockdown. This included creating products for teenagers to purchase PlayStation games; and for

---

14 L Gonçalves, *Organisational Mastery: The product development blueprint for executive leaders* (Rethink Press, 2019)

the parents, enabling integrations with local online sellers so that the checkout would be seamless. In just two weeks they reacted quickly to a dramatic change in market conditions and completely reshaped and re-aligned the organisation to meet the new demands of the market.

This suits smaller organisations, old and new, since larger ones operate with less flexibility and are not always able to respond as quickly. Using the quarterly cadence I've described, it's easier to adapt the OKRs and portfolio with maximum flexibility that will get the product or service to market quickly and boost the chances of survival. I refer to OKRs as the heartbeat of the entire organisation because they enable everyone to be fully aligned and working at the same pace. For those traditional companies that don't adapt in this way, it's like running a race with lead weights on their shoes – before long, they'll find themselves outpaced and left far behind the competition.

OKRs should:

- Specifically answer what the organisation wants to achieve within a determined time-frame (eg after a year or quarter)

- Serve as the strategic theme or the 'burning imperative' (as some companies call it) that overarch what the organisation wants to accomplish

- Be qualitative, supported by a set of actionable steps or key objectives

- Be measurable, with between one to five key results

Reduce time to market

A consequence of companies optimised for efficiency are that they are optimised for both speed and value delivery for their customers. When you commit to properly implementing OKRs, you are implementing objective and key results for products, where customers are at the centre and you define the product for them. It's a straightforward question: What do you want to achieve for the customer? To improve customer satisfaction, or to meet the needs of the customer?

A traditional organisation would set about fulfilling these goals by assigning projects to individual departments, for example, research and development, finance, marketing, etc. The result leads to optimisation *only* in those separate silos and not across the entire organisation. This is a slow, cumbersome and often fractious exercise that inhibits a quick release into the market. In the digital age, thinking needs to shift towards focusing on products and not projects, in which talent from different areas is involved as one team. This may initially meet with some resistance, for example, a marketing executive may raise concerns that they then need to involve themselves in several product startups. Each product will also need specified roles and positions filled, so it will require creating individual product teams with the requisite skills and expertise drawn from across different departments almost from day one to realise fulfilment. The organisation will bear an initial personnel cost increase as the products become populated with dedicated team members, but this is offset because the products have been optimised for speed and can be released into the market iteratively, generating incremental income.

It's the opposite mindset of optimising for cost efficiency, where the marketing exec sits on the outside of the product in a central silo. This creates a barrier to speed. Where the product is populated by all the necessary team members, the barrier is broken. What this effectively shows is that the level of interdependencies in an organisation is usually greater than anyone first imagines; but in an optimised environment they can be streamlined, and every team member's capabilities are mined to the max. Once the paradigm has shifted, you will want to build more products and replicate team expertise in each. Once again, the cost of salaries will initially increase as a result (you may have to recruit new talent into the organisation to fulfil those roles), but the speed at which those products reach the market will increase exponentially. The revenue generated by that product will compensate the cost of the salaries.

The point is, always look at what it is your customer is trying to solve or what it is they need (even if they don't know it yet). The natural ease of OKRs is that they highlight the various products of the organisation. Following the first couple of quarterly OKRs, the logical next step is to migrate from the old way to the new way in creating individual product mini startups, or an entirely product-focused organisation, and dispensing with the need for departments. Apart from the obvious benefit of reducing times to market, the focus is clearly and continually aimed at the customer, with whom the product maintains an ongoing relationship on a regular basis. It keeps the product fresh, relevant and exciting. It also keeps the customer engaged. In a worldwide crisis or when you're trying to stand out from your customers in a digitally crowded marketplace, presence and visibility are key. Each time you create a new product, bear the Product pillar of the ADAPT Methodology® in mind to remind you of your strategic approach.

Continuous improvement

Some years ago, I noticed that when people at team level identified various problems, the solutions were invariably strangled by internal politics. That's because many executives are completely unaware of problems and politics that sit beneath their noses and so the problems never get addressed or solved. I've seen how teams evaluate why and how the problems arise and then work diligently to solve them – but rarely from an organisational perspective. Usually, these problems can't be managed alone because the solutions require support from higher management. This is when the traditional structure reveals its barriers and the lack of executive support brings the whole issue to a full stop: delays, waiting for authorisation, infighting and indifference. This isn't a 'people problem', it's a structural one. It wasn't until I read Jason Little's *Lean Change Management Approach*[15] that I had my own lightbulb moment: change doesn't happen if you force it on people, but it *will* happen when people are allowed to collaborate in problem solving, thus *co*-creating change. I've since enhanced and incorporated this thinking into my own practice with my clients by asking executives to create a coalition with their employees. Traditionally, executives would delegate this task, but in so doing, they remain removed from the process. What I ask them to do is to own it and drive it using an impediment organisational board, which is nothing more than a formal way to identity, and then to escalate, issues that are not visible to the organisation. The immediate benefit is that this creates a channel of communication for people caught in the middle of the organisation who have previously had no platform to raise problems. The coalition enables these problems to become visible to the executives who frequently are unaware that such

15 J Little, *Lean Change Management: Innovative practices for managing organizational change* (Happy Melly Express, 2014)

problems exist. This coalition is extremely important because it connects them to their frontline operators and encourages them to co-create a solution. Its success lies in the fact that executives have the power to authorise change, but the team members have the deep operational knowledge of what causes the problems. Listening and sharing ideas are used to work through the possible solutions to co-create change for everyone. Sometimes that might be the simplest solution to a problem that has become tangled up in departmental bureaucracy. For example, I was once consulting with an engineer organisation of 2,000 employees. I needed to print out materials, but because I wasn't an employee, I didn't have authorisation to use a printer. Every consultant had to follow this protocol and continually interrupt team members' flow just to carry out a simple print task. It was frustrating for everyone concerned and resulted in many wasted hours of nonproductive output for the organisation. When we calculated what this meant in real terms, the figure was an eye-watering €300,000 loss each year. Nothing we could say could shift the problem because at middle management level the response was always the same: 'These are the rules.' The solution was simple. We placed the problem on an organisational impediment board (used to collect impediments, so that the team can then meet and discuss how to overcome these) and invited the chief information officer to participate. Once he realised that the cost to the organisation was significant, he immediately distributed an email to the management team that changed the rule by granting external consultants the permission to print without the need for authorisation. Having given the issue top line visibility, the rule was broken and the problem was fixed. It wasn't about blaming middle management, because they were simply following the process. It was the structure that prevented visibility across all levels that lay at the heart of it. Only an executive level decision can change some rules, so unless executives are involved in these conversations, impediments will always exist. Ultimately this approach costs businesses money. It's in every executive's grasp to enable change for their organisation to operate more efficiently and more productively to increase output and turn products around more quickly to release them into market. However, they must engage in more conversations, listen to middle management and frontline workers, and share ideas to drive continuous improvement.

Knowledge sharing

As many executives will know, the battle to recruit the best talent is a tough fight to win and it's not always possible to fill key positions with external candidates. The solution is to use the people that they already have in-house.

Knowledge sharing is one of the most important practices any organisation should adopt to avoid the talent war. It must apply to all, the executive team included, yet it's one of the most underused tools that many businesses overlook. It's not something that can be implemented overnight because silo structures (departments and/or projects) build communication barriers and prevent sharing knowledge. At a basic level, this begins with team members asking themselves if they have enough knowledge to perform their daily tasks. If not, how will knowledge sharing between *all* teams better equip them to deliver meaningful impact upon the business? Without the space within an organisation for knowledge sharing, there can be little or no hope of achieving change.

When I refer to knowledge sharing, I specifically mean implementing informal communities of practice within an organisation. If you adopt my approach of a product-centric business, you will break the barriers created by silos/departments and the whole organisation will be the beneficiary of knowledge sharing. It's an intense, exciting process that helps to remind people of their higher purpose, and where the outcome results in increased knowledge and quality-driven solutions discovered through collective sharing of input and ideas. Team members simultaneously learn from one another and contribute towards making a positive impact upon the flow of the team's ability to deliver the product they're attached to. More significantly, it reduces decision-making delays because teams are no longer dependent on top-level authorisation.

The four levels I recommend implementing are:

1. **Team:** Team members sharing with their direct team colleagues

2. **Product:** Team sharing with other teams inside of the same product

3. **Organisational:** Sharing of best practices, anecdotes, problems, solutions with cross-product teams

4. **External:** Attending outside events/conferences/ meetups to exchange learning, problems and solutions, with opportunities to recruit

Team level

First, encourage team members to establish a collective reading of business titles. Sharing the stand-out points raised among the team is not only a powerful way to bond people together, it also encourages co-creative thinking which can assist with problem solving. Titles can vary from any business book in sectors relevant to your own, or ones that provide insight into best practice. Team building, sales techniques, fresh approaches or new trends and techniques – each will generate discussion and spark ideas where the ultimate direct benefit will be delivering the best product solutions for customers. Second, facilitate informal sessions during which product teams can share ideas about processes and operations. Just as importantly, these sessions are also a time to listen and learn from those in the team with specialist product knowledge who want to teach the group a new technique or explain an aspect of a product in detail that everyone would benefit from. It's also a highly effective way to retain talent as they feel valued and that their contribution to the business really does make a difference.

Product level

The purpose here is to pool knowledge, experience and best practice to discover solutions to common problems that would traditionally be worked through in isolation. An isolated approach multiplied across numerous products is a costly and time-consuming exercise. Knowledge sharing on a product level significantly reduces both and removes old barriers. It allows space for crucial conversations between everyone to raise collective issues and solve problems together when once they might have been hesitant in making unilateral decisions. Sharing knowledge in this way creates a group of people that are super-aligned, who fully understand each other's competencies and agree with what they want to achieve.

Organisational level

The cadence planning I've suggested earlier allows the space and opportunities within the three-monthly cycles to share knowledge and information with the whole organisation. Each OKR and portfolio management three-monthly cycle has its own focus in which the organisation's 'big picture' is shared to collectively agree its overall goals and then be fed into the organisation's knowledge bank. This allows for group creative and objective thinking, where a contribution from one product teams may offer an insight about issues that arise in another.

External level

It's always useful to step into the outside world to see how other people are working and what they do. External meetups represent exciting opportunities to meet with fellow professionals from other organisations and are also ideal to showcase the best parts of your own organisation. Ideas, best practice and knowledge can be shared among business peers which can then be taken back into your own business for further sharing and implementation. With your HR in attendance, external meetups (eg, conferences) are an excellent way to recruit the best talent, and these events can form an active part of a focused recruitment strategy. This can save a business thousands in advertising costs and recruitment fees over the course of a year. For example, a typical head-hunting agency will charge 15–20% of a successful candidate's annual salary in commission. Multiply that over eight to ten new recruits per year and the savings made are significant.

Innovation

Most companies ultimately fail because they don't have any kind of innovation strategy or perceived budget in place, yet innovation is crucial for future survival. The fast-paced digital era is a breeding ground for new competitors to appear on the scene and threaten your product's market share. These are businesses that don't follow the traditional rules of bigger companies – they're disruptors and are fuelled by innovation. This has many executive leaders of established organisations seriously worried that they're stuck in their old ways without the right tools to keep them both competitive and relevant in the marketplace – and rightly so. The risk in ignoring innovation is that products can become obsolete and irrelevant. The banking sector has seen several established brands outsmarted by disruptors that have created innovative technological features that directly appeal to the changing needs of their customers. For example, the disruptors have dispensed with time-wasting communications (by letter) when requesting PINs or applying monthly administrative account fees. Disruptors have introduced numerous smart solutions that allow customers to be connected to their accounts with instant outcomes and at their convenience. Many of the older, established brands are having to play catch-up to retain, or win, new clients.

Committing space, energy, time and resources to innovation is key to any business's survival. To facilitate innovation, I recommend design thinking, which although not a new concept, proves to be effective time and again. More specifically, using tools created by Google Ventures as the Design Sprint, it's possible to go from having an idea to moving rapidly on to releasing a prototype into the market for validation from customers. The key to deliverability, however, lies in the scheduling. Although design thinking is used by many businesses that would consider themselves digital-era fit for purpose, they don't fully optimise their organisational flow sufficiently enough, and this is where my approach differentiates. I've seen many large organisations employ Design Sprint when it comes to innovation, but what often happens is that their ideas are not implemented because they become trapped by the backlog of their own day-to-day operations. My solution to clear the backlog is by allocating one week for innovation at the end of each quarterly cycle, during which new ideas are tested and validated. By the end of that week, it's possible that one idea stands out above the rest which could generate revenue and is worth pursuing. As the next quarterly cycle, begins, that idea is folded into portfolio management and OKRs from which the financial objectives are created immediately to pursue the innovation developed in the previous week. This creates a cadence of planning that always integrates innovation that is in complete alignment with the quarterly *and* overall business strategy. Each quarter begins with new innovation objectives where the budget for it is already assigned. Unlike the traditional, project-led companies who take a gamble by spending twelve months developing new products that might not even meet evolving customer needs by the time they are released into a steeped market, enabling new products to be released into the market quickly to generate revenue faster is a game changer in respect of enabling innovation to be integrated with the strategy.

The figure below shows the entire blueprint. This is described in detail in my book *Organisational Mastery*.[16]

Summary

If I've been at all persuasive up until this point, you may well be thinking that you need to make some changes within your organisation. Even if your business has a healthy turnover or your product is digital dependent, you might now be identifying numerous gaps that need to be filled. The good news is, not everything I've mentioned in the five-pillar ADAPT Methodology® needs to be accomplished at the same time. However, you might now be prompted to ask: 'Where is my organisation at this moment?'

---

16 L Gonçalves, *Organisational Mastery: The product development blueprint for executive leaders* (Rethink Press, 2019)

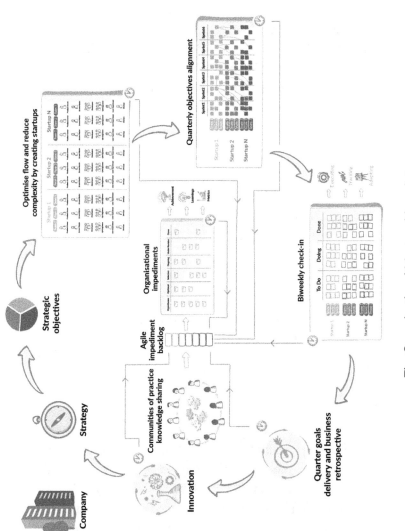

Company · **Strategy** · **Strategic objectives**

Optimise flow and reduce complexity by creating startups

Startup 1 · Startup 2 · Startup N

Quarterly objectives alignment

Sprint1 Sprint2 Sprint3 Sprint4 Sprint5 Sprint6

Startup 1 · Startup 2 · Startup N

Achievement · Knowledge · Metrics

Organisational impediments

Objectives · Options · Selection · Ongoing · Value Realise · Done

Communities of practice knowledge sharing

Agile impediment backlog

Innovation

Biweekly check-in

To Do · Doing · Done

Startup 1 · Startup 2 · Startup N

Executing · Tracking · Adapting

Quarter goals delivery and business retrospective

The Organisational Mastery blueprint

My personal recommendation is to think about the OKRs first, because this always makes the greatest initial impact on my clients. This is where executives see how and why flow is important; OKRs unlock the flow that then leads one into the next and they then begin to connect. Even if yours is a digital organisation, ask yourself these same questions in respect of how well you connect your daily operations to strategy while ensuring that everyone is aligned:

- Are you able to shift gears and direction, as I've described, every quarter?

- Are you optimised for speed, or are you optimising for cost efficiency?

- Are you able to share knowledge within the organisation?

- Are you able to identify the problems that delay you and hurt you?

- Are you able to create sustainable innovation every quarter?

I understand that for many traditional, long-established businesses, these may be difficult questions to ask; the responses may be even more difficult to initially confront. But think back to when you began this book – if you were worried about the prospects and survivability of your business, then this chapter alone should encourage you to energetically embrace the transformation your business needs. The ADAPT

Methodology® in its entirety, when planned and implemented in full, offers the outline of a roadmap to adapting your business to become more viable, more profitable, more relevant and more visible to your customers.

✔▬ In the Transformation segment you have been
● ▬ prompted to think about how well you have designed your organisation and aligned its long-term vision to meet the future needs of customers and continually changing market conditions. If you haven't yet taken the scorecard, you might want to measure how successful you will be as a digital leader now:

⊕ http://bit.ly/Scorecard_ADAPT_Book

SIX

The Glue

I hope to have now raised awareness of the five crucial areas I consider that executives need to address for their businesses to survive long into the digital era. This chapter will explain the practical measures to drive that outcome. These are relatable and applicable to any business, irrespective of the sector it operates in – from retail, manufacturing, software development or financial services to B2B providers of all kinds. I will outline how to build the top layer that will transform any business into a digital organisation that connects to, and is ready, for the digital world. There is nothing in the following that suggests executives need to change their core business. The state of mind thinking I've encouraged all to embrace will instead act as an additional 'plug-in' that connects the dots, where each feeds into the other.

The top layer that binds the whole organisation so that it links directly to both products and customers requires creating a digital strategy. It is the glue, and for that to be effective and hold strong, each of the five pillars of the ADAPT Methodology® need careful examination to identify where the gaps are and how they can be filled. In some areas they may be bigger than others, but if the digital layer isn't made whole, the transformation will be incomplete and open to future vulnerabilities.

Many high street retailers continue to canvas consumers using traditional mass market, non-customised print methods such as newspaper and TV advertisements or flyers and brochures delivered to many thousands of homes. This blanket approach is the non-digital format of spam – easily ignored and disposable. There are some practical measures exec-utives can take to begin their journey towards their business digital transformation.

Create a content strategy

This is an approach that I have successfully employed in my own business development. It's an easy first step because it relies on what you already know and what you do. Creating relevant content that educates and informs your customers about your products, services and about what your business stands for provides customers with enormous additional value over and above what you sell. Consumers crave interesting and engaging content over advertising, and in today's world where they check their mobile devices up to 150 times a day, it's key that your business stands out and is visible.[17] In so doing, you are facilitating the potential for significantly increased customer development. This includes helping them solve some of their problems even before they purchase from you by producing a series of short, instructional 'how to' videos related to your business which share tips and useful insights (eg assembling tables, fixing a leak, building a garden wall, restoring furniture, cooking their favourite recipe, etc). These tutorials work well online because they offer scope to scale, but also broaden your own horizons by inviting customers to further educational workshops and talks. Featuring the range of products you sell in the tutorials is a persuasive driver for the customer to then purchase those items from you, especially if you include an incentive such as a discount code (you can then track those that convert into sales).

In essence, you are telling a story that engages your end user, whichever sector your business trades

---

17 J Brandon, 'The surprising reason millennials check their phones 150 times a day', *Inc.* (17 April 2017), www.inc.com/john-brandon/science-says-this-is-the-reason-millennials-check-their-phones-150-times-per-day.html, accessed 1 April 2021

in. Through storytelling, you harness the power of persuasion that then aligns customers to your brand, driving traffic to your products via social media such as YouTube and Instagram. The important difference overall is that you shift from blanket advertising of goods and services to tailoring your marketing efforts via educating the customer about those goods and services using a higher level of segmentation. As a result, you appeal directly to customer interest: instead of selling the product, you sell the solution to their problem. Even if they fail to make a purchase straight away, you will have made your mark and your brand will be lodged in their mind with a greater chance of preference. I cannot recommend this shift from gambling with a mass market approach to feeding a mass demand for content enough. Not through selling, but through education, education, education – and offering it at no charge.

Data

Data is what every organisation collects for the insights and information it gathers. As the Covid-19 pandemic demonstrated, however, where that knowledge is limited to the financials or stock control, businesses are missing opportunities to monitor and respond to shifting market conditions. Businesses that harvest data in more connected ways enables them to analyse and predict customer purchasing behaviours and patterns that offer them a greatly increased competitive advantage. Breaking data out of its silos and connecting it to all departments shows how the entire customer journey is connected across all streams of the organisation. The results of that analysis then drive improvement in respect of products, customer experience and service. They also optimise operations and result in significant cost savings. Without a deeper analysis of this cross-integration, businesses will lack those important insights. For example, a warehousing system for a retail business could benefit from a link to a long-range weather app which more accurately predicts consumer demand far enough in advance to order or reprioritise existing stock. Be that wet-weather gear, outdoor leisure clothing and equipment or seasonally adjusted food and beverages, the stock levels could reflect the peaks and troughs of customer behaviours as predicted by patterns revealed in the data. It reduces the risk of relying on assumed annual seasonal fluctuations that, in an ever-changing environmental climate, are less predictable.

A fully integrated data strategy designed by a specialist is an important investment worth making because the cost of implementation will soon be mitigated in the operational efficiencies and savings. For customers, it also facilitates a direct and personalised approach once their purchasing patterns and behaviours become clearer, arising from data. For example, if a customer regularly purchases a particular product, the collected data allows the retailer to enhance their experience by alerting them to any promotions and discounts they would then benefit from, and where appropriate, offer to deliver it direct to their door without the need to visit the store in person (useful during a pandemic). Similarly, for those customers that regularly shop online, data can suggest items to pre-fill their shopping cart based on their previous history.

Using data imaginatively creates stand-out customer service opportunities where the goal is not only to encourage regular and repeat business, but also to alert when that customer seems to drop away. What this data might suggest is that they have begun to shop elsewhere, at which point you can send a targeted promotion by text/email/push notification (assuming they have opted in previously) to encourage them to return. As every business knows, acquiring new customers is always the most expensive element in marketing terms, but retaining them is considerably less so. The ambition is to spend less on constantly attracting new customers (such as expensive mass marketing techniques) while ensuring that you use data to keep those you already have. When you consider that every business possesses data about its customers, it makes complete sense to use the insights it offers to its full potential by implementing a data strategy along the lines I have suggested.

Agility

If you are an executive of a software development company, you're probably already employing some form of Agile (Scrum, Kanban, etc) to develop your digital projects, although you may be scratching your head and wondering what all the hype was about, especially if you've not seen the results you were expecting. Note that I refer to 'projects', which as you will know from reading the Agility pillar, is not where I recommend focusing your energy. Agile is too often implemented as a tick-box exercise and sits within departmental teams (in silos) where, despite best intentions, it becomes bound by the end-focus, project-centric pressures of the Waterfall approach. Traditional companies that lack experience of operating fully in the digital era (including those that create digital 'solutions' such as online stores, websites, apps, etc) still arrange their operations around Waterfall methodology, taking months to develop and validate ideas at great expense only to realise limited, or no, ROI at the end of the process when 100% of the product is released to market.

Agile thrives when employed in a *product* orientated mindset, as I've described. Implementing it, as outlined in Chapter 3, releases 5% of the product idea but with 100% implementation. The iterative Agile approach and incremental customer/end user validation provides ongoing commentary on how that product can be continually improved while reducing risk of a catastrophic end-of-project failure. Nobody wants their products to fall off a cliff edge. With my product-focused approach, whenever a product team experiences an iterative problem, there's space, energy and resources available to resolve it while still generating revenue.

In practical terms, using Waterfall could see a business allocate thousands of its budget in creating an amazing, bells and whistles web shop developed over a whole year only to discover that the customer only makes use of 20% of its features (it's common knowledge among the software development community that up to 80% of features are never used).[18] That's 80% of wasted output and wasted budget. It would have been better to have begun the process by building a functional, basic web shop that was iteratively improved every two weeks, adding in new features validated by customer feedback and needs. It's the same principle that has witnessed the evolution of the iPhone, which on first release was as basic as basic could be compared to the highly sophisticated (and continually improving) versions we regularly see released to market. At the centre of this Agile approach, Apple is serving the customer within a highly competitive market, discovering what features work best for them, those that don't and what they'd like to see included in future releases.

---

18 T Taulli, 'Are most of your product's features… useless?', *Forbes* (24 February 2019), www.forbes.com/sites/tomtaulli/2019/02/24/are-most-of-your-products-features-useless/?sh=789100944599, accessed 1 April 2021

Every business can replicate this approach across its product range, from a small physical goods manufacturer, software development company to a single shop or multi-chain retailer. Incremental release into the market increases the product's intuitive understanding of what the customer needs (often before the customer knows it) and helps you be more aligned with your customers while enabling continuous validation. Once the realisation sets in that Agile isn't simply a tick-box, project enabler, this opens the door towards your implementing and translating it incredibly powerfully into your daily operations.

Product

Linked intrinsically to each pillar of the ADAPT Methodology,® product development in the digital era requires a complete strategy that permeates the whole business. Such a strategy will invariably be driven by customer demand and need for new, existing and future products. I've already explained that product is a state of mind, and it's from that standpoint that a business can really begin to take great leaps forward. We must strategise product in a completely different way if those leaps are to be achieved.

For example, when we think about creating a website, often that is as far as the thinking evolves – that because an online store front exists within a digital landscape, it will be the answer to all our problems. However, unless it stands out from the crowd, it will be invisible. Regard that website as a product (in the same way as physical products or services) with a complete strategy that develops and validates user-friendly features that drive sales, and a whole series of possibilities open up that will serve the customers' needs in dynamic ways. Your website product demands the same care and attention as the goods and service your business aims to sell. The strategy must include answers to the following questions:

- What are the goals and objectives?

- What's the budget?

- What needs to be implemented to make it happen?

Planning a complete strategy from day one allows innovation in design, thinking, innovation, testing and improvement. The website will ultimately then be populated with features, apps and desirable tools that customers will return to repeatedly with confidence. However, that's only the public-facing element of the strategy. A complete strategy will also include how the business then follows this through, and seamlessly so.

For example, if your business is a retail concern, your online shopping website (remember, this is a product) might have the best, user-friendly features (also each developed as separate products that interface with the website) that rank highly with the customer at the front end of their transaction journey with you. These can be anything from a suggested shopping list, offering recommendations or giving discounts based on their previous purchasing behaviours, but the journey is not over until the customer receives their goods. Always bear in mind that no matter how fantastic your ultimate products are (the goods you sell), if the delivery element falls short of customer expectations, they won't care how great it is – their perception of the business will be tainted by poor after-sales service.

A number of retailers have found innovative solutions to this by developing apps (and thinking of them as products) which are designed to help their delivery drivers plan the best routes or avoid traffic blackspots. These apps have been planned iteratively over many months of testing and execution in MVP format, and incrementally improved following feedback from their drivers (ie the 'customers' of the app) as to their economic efficiency (time and fuel usage) and reliability. The data received from these apps plays a vital role in being able to understand and predict when traffic is at its heaviest and where accidents and delays most frequently occur, thus providing valuable insights to these businesses that are all designed to increase their chances of profitability and survival in the digital era.

The practical application of any product strategy is that it should not be developed in isolation – buried within, for example, the marketing or IT departments alone and labelled as a project. Each product (website, apps, payment features, etc) needs to be developed as if it were a startup, populated with a whole team of expertise to support it and connected to the over-arching strategy of the business. Each product represents a value stream, not simply a function, because each contributes to the long-term, connected health of the business. Product as a state of mind sits at the core of the transformation layer.

Transformation

In Chapter 5, I wrote about the transformation layer in terms of it being similar to an essential plug-in that will prompt executives to rethink their whole approach. While I'm certain that a vast majority of businesses already own websites (as store fronts for whichever sector they operate in) and employ some form of in-house software developers, it doesn't necessarily follow that they're best calibrated to take full advantage of the digital era. As with product, I want to help you rethink the way you develop the *entire* organisation, which also means viewing it completely differently. To begin with:

- Be flexible in your thinking.

- Be open to more agility than you already are.

Then, examine how you can begin to work towards organisational mastery:

- Structure your organisation away from functional departments and projects towards thinking in terms of value streams and products.

- Create organisational impediment boards to collect impediments, so that these can be dealt with and removed.

- Use OKRs to help the business react, respond and change at a faster pace.

- Be at the heart of facilitating the business to continuously improve.

- Create a coalition between managers, leaders and operational people.

- Use all the knowledge within your company to empower everyone to grow.

- Facilitate communities of practices throughout the whole business where your people can discuss issues, problems and concerns with each other.

- Implement design thinking methodologies that are highly incorporated into the quarterly cycles that enable ongoing, core incremental innovation.

Now you'll be at the forefront of creating an organisation fit for the digital era which embraces innovation at its core – agile and flexible enough to develop, test, validate and continually improve at a rate faster than you had ever imagined possible. In reality, none of this is an instant fix for long-standing issues that may well have contributed to a decline in sales and performance, but any business that undertakes the transformation I've outlined here and adapts themselves using the framework and tools I've described has a fighting chance at survival. Without doubt, it's a long journey, but the good news is, not every aspect needs to be tackled at the same time. Many businesses' executives will already have many of the pieces in place, but all will certainly benefit from revisiting and reviewing in the round to see how they connect.

For those businesses currently structured along the traditional, industrial-age models I described in Chapter 1, I suggest re-reading the Approach pillar as this requires the least amount of organisational change. Simply implementing some new ideas in how to approach customers differently is the beginning of a shift in mindset that any executive can be proud of, especially as they'll immediately witness the results of that change.

Similarly, if you then turn your attention to the volumes of data your business already collects but underutilises, once you decide to develop an integrated strategy with the help of specialists, that data can be put to work and answer the questions you have about your customers' purchasing patterns and behaviours. Data will also offer up some insights that may surprise you, and if you respond to these, your customers may notice your brand over the competition more.

Summary

Only when you've taken the necessary measures to implement the Approach and Data pillars can you begin to think about the Agility, Product and Transformation pillars, when you will need to shift your mindset further to embrace the need for a physical organisational change in the way your organisation operates, and even in its design. These areas are where traditional businesses are outsmarted and outsold by their direct, digital-age-savvy competitors, as well as by the hundreds of startups that appear in their sector annually. Your business must be ready, willing and able to adapt to the digital age if it's to claim its rightful market share, and ultimately, to survive.

The scorecard below will invite you to complete a new scorecard. Even if your organisation has implemented Agile, you may now be wondering if you have gone far enough yourself. Simply delegating and not participating will not work, and in time your significant investment will be for nothing. Have you, as a leader, fully engaged with Agile and applied it to your own role? At this point I'd invite you to refer to a separate scorecard that measures your own leader-ship roadmap. Depending on your responses, it may prompt you to re-evaluate Agile in its entirety and consider how implementing the Agile methodology will best serve you. Completing this scorecard bench-marks your ability to build a successful digital product organisation. It identifies opportunities for leveraged growth and will inform you if you will succeed as a modern leader:

⊕ https://organisationalmastery.com/scorecard

SEVEN

Avoiding The Most Common Mistakes

The biggest mistake most executive leaders make is allowing their fear of digital transformation to prevent a partial, or complete implementation (especially if they're uncertain as to what it really is) or by appointing the wrong people to oversee it. Intellectually, they understand the rationale that necessitates digital transformation to remain competitive and maintain market share, but they are concerned that they don't know how to achieve this comprehensively. One of the most common mistakes I see when executives embark on a path towards digital transformation is an overall lack of organisational consensus of what that digital transformation is, and the aims it's trying to achieve. The temptation is to embark upon the transformation, ring-fenced by budgetary constraints, in either a half-hearted, piece-meal fashion by doing it themselves (and without the requisite experience) or by appointing a trusted, well-known consultancy that may not be the ideal exponent of such transformations themselves. In this chapter I will outline some of the most frequent errors that executive leaders make, alongside solutions that will enable them to fully implement digital transformation within their organisations.

Digital transformation is a fad

For many leaders, developing and implementing a digital-age-fit strategy sits outside of their experience. It has only been readily taught at university level in recent years. Without guidance and insight, it's more difficult to understand why it's necessary to adopt a different mindset in the ways I've described throughout this book. Traditional practices and industrial-age pre-conditioning predicate their natural inclination to default to their version of 'normal' – operating in functional, project-led departments. The major misconception is in believing that digital is a fad, one that will soon be replaced by yet another. In addition to this, the fact that nobody in the organisation can agree on what digital means leads to a myriad of conflicting viewpoints and directions of travel. This lack of cohesive, strategic thinking always ends in failure and only serves to confirm their worst suspicions that digital is little more than new-fangled baloney that doesn't deliver results. The plea I hear most is, 'We don't know what we're doing,' and under these circumstances, I agree. The ADAPT Methodology® provides a concrete definition of 'digital transformation' that acts as that springboard towards comprehending the issues raised and then gives ways of responding to them. The five pillars I describe provide the blueprint to create a digital transformation in any organisation that will both nourish it from within and drive results to ensure it remains relevant, not just now, but for the years ahead. My blueprint isn't prescriptive, but by following and adhering to the principles I've identified as essential, it's possible for any business leader to embark on revisiting their vision as it relates to their core business to create direction that everyone can align themselves to.

It's the IT department's responsibility

If the IT team isn't connected to the overall strategy that translates to the daily operations, it runs the real risk of developing a product that is entirely unsuitable for, or unwanted by, customers. The IT team needs to be as invested in the OKRs and product development as any other departmental team, and they must remain focused on creating value streams and how they contribute to the entire organisation. Ensure you create value streams and products through a completely cross-functional approach where teams from each different department are involved. This increases the possibility of transforming the entire organisation at the same time.

Creating a digital transformation silo

Establishing a dedicated digital transformation project management office (PMO) is not the answer. This only creates another silo that remains disconnected from the rest of the organisation. Where once a PMO was the nerve centre of an organisation in driving projects forward, its members now operate by using an embedded, traditional, project-led mindset that's incompatible with thinking of product as a 'state of mind'. Digital transformation will fail if housed within a PMO silo. Instead, appoint an executive team member to assume the responsibility of chief digital officer that will lead the transformation across the whole organisation. The officer can then engage expert, external digital consultants (see Chapter 8) that remain neutral and uninvolved in any internal conflicts or politics. Let these consultants help to develop the strategy and to create and incrementally test and analyse the relevant value streams and products. They will then expand this across the entire organisation step by step.

Transformation is a small project that can be implemented all at once

The temptation is to implement digital transformation across the organisation totally and quickly. But where an organisation employs a large amount of people, the challenge is too large to implement the digital transformation effectively all at once and it will not be successful. It's better to introduce this on a gradual basis, creating a few small startup groups at a time, which can identity their own OKRs that are aligned with the overall strategy. They then develop small-step initiatives and value streams via manageable chunks during which you can establish communities of practice and shared knowledge across the whole organisation. If you attempt this all at once, there are no opportunities to incrementally share this knowledge, risking the same mistakes repeating within each group.

Digital transformation is not a small project. It's a complete game changer that, in time, will reinvent how an organisation operates. Implementing it requires a complete paradigm shift in mindset and focus, as the ADAPT Methodology® suggests – a shift that becomes embedded into executives' day-to-day operations and knowledge of the business. That will take time, not just six months, not even one year. This is systemic and radical incremental change that will impact the organisation over two or more years. That vision takes commitment, and it must be assigned as a priority with the appropriate budget to match. A spendthrift approach is a wasted effort.

Failing to listen to the data

Most organisations don't know how to interpret the data they collect, so the data they amass doesn't contribute towards any discernible outcomes. They are also uncertain how to establish an integrated data strategy that offers them the three key insights I have outlined in Chapter 2 (improving service, improving knowledge about customer behaviours and improving business operations). The solution is to engage an external data expert (see Chapter 8) to help them create and implement a cohesive strategy that will generate and analyse data. The insights of various data streams will then reveal more information, not only about customers, but also about where the business needs to invest in particular areas more than others.

Losing sight of creating value

Focusing on expense alone fails to provide the complete picture. Results are not always immediately apparent, so if a chief financial officer (CFO) focuses on operational costs alone, it is difficult to measure value. For example, most still regard IT engineering as a huge cost for the company without necessarily appreciating that it's a critical business enabler. If a CFO only examines the numbers in isolation on a departmental basis, they are more likely to look to make cuts to costs if they don't consider the value each contributes to the value streams generated. This approach will destroy the digital transformation. The solution is to recruit an experienced chief digital officer who then has complete oversight of the strategy.

Lack of executive team involvement

Often, executives believe that they can simply delegate driving the digital transformation by hiring an expert that then reports to them each month. This approach doesn't constitute involvement; instead, it's total detachment from the aims and objectives of gradually but completely redesigning the entire organisation that impacts on each department. When the CEO or senior executives are uninvolved, the transformation will fail. It's vital that they are as involved as every other person in the business, because not only will they have their finger on the pulse of change, but they have the authority to make informed decisions to drive that change forward. Simply delegating, receiving a monthly report and not being an example of that change will mean the digital transformation will fail. The need for executive ownership is a top priority because it clearly shows the whole organisation that they are completely connected to the transformation and overall strategy. It inspires.

Inward thinking

Frequently, organisations undertaking any form of major transformation focus on their own objectives rather than analysing their customers' needs. As a result, they lose sight of their customer database and fail to validate what they are producing. However, it's vital *at all times* to maintain and nurture those relationships with customers by placing them right at the centre of all developments and to continue that validation process. The solution lies in employing any one of the many design thinking tools that are available.

The wrong person to lead digital transformation

I'm frequently shocked when it's apparent that whoever is appointed as chief digital officer to drive the digital transformation lacks the correct skills. Often, it's a newly created role for an executive to justify their continuation in the business, but that person lacks relevant, or even practical, experience of the digital landscape. If it's necessary, or unavoidable, to appoint internally, then the very least qualification should be knowledge of the digital landscape. Ideally, appoint an external expert; but never appoint anyone who clearly has no experience.

Excluding everyone from co-creating transformation

The 'command and control' mentality belongs to the past. If digital transformation is to be successful, it cannot be the result of a top-down push of issuing commands that need to be obeyed. That doesn't lead to a happy environment and will only reinforce barriers. The way ahead begins with the leadership team having agreed the need for digital transformation. At an operational level, enabling and empowering people to co-create the necessary changes in a coalition at all levels, following the agreed direction, fully facilitates the process in total alignment with the overall strategy.

Managers not visionaries leading the transformation

Most digital transformation initiatives fail because companies have managers managing the transformation rather than entrepreneurs leading it.

In my experience, people who are great at managing operations are usually not great at disrupting the status quo. Even worse, I believe they possess the opposite skill set. Many times, I've heard the following from managers responsible for leading digital transformations:

- 'Luís, you are bringing in too many changes too fast. You need to slow down.'

- 'Luís, this is not the way we do things around here.'

- 'Luís, you don't understand. We're different and our reality is much more complicated than that.'

One company even rejected my proposal to help them with their digital transformation by saying our proposal was too disruptive!

I have a message for these people: you need to change fast and adapt to survive. There is no such thing as 'too disruptive' in today's world. Now is not the time to manage a change – it's time to lead a transformation.

Not changing a company's reward system

Are you killing your organisation by rewarding people that do not want change?

Some time ago I had the chance to meet an old friend who was CEO of a Singapore-based company, and he explained that he was in trouble. He confessed that the company's digital transformation was failing because the company was set up in a way that rewarded people that do not want to change. He believes that 99% of companies are like this.

He explained to me that if, as an employee, you do not try something disruptive, you do not break anything, and in three to four years you'll get a promotion. On the other hand, if you try to do things in a different way, it's likely that, in the beginning at least, you will not get optimal results and you'll be seen as a failure. So by trying to do things differently, you are putting your career progress at risk.

If you are a leader, ask yourself how you are building your organisation to succeed in the digital era. Are you rewarding people that don't want to take chances, or the ones that try to create innovative solutions to take your company to the next level?

Another problem that I see in organisations is when their bonus system is attached to employee performance. Usually, this stifles any culture of innovation, leading to employees doing the same old stuff over and over. By attaching bonuses to staff salaries, you are telling people there is no space for mistakes, because the only thing that matters is 'their performance'. People will be scared to try anything new because failing means not receiving their bonus.

So many leaders want to undergo a digital transformation but still run the company using outdated 'carrot and stick' policies. In this case, if you want to drive innovation, you need to support people to take chances and behave in different ways, not drive people to do thing in the same old ways.

Designing a company based on industrial-era principles

It's interesting to see how many leaders want to implement a digital transformation to adapt their company to the digital age but keep running their company based on principles of an industrial age.

Today's managers were taught to design a company to be optimised for costs and not the speed of delivery. This mindset comes from the industrial era, when the priority was to produce the most material possible for the lowest possible cost. So the entire company was optimised for cost efficiency.

In the digital era, the paradigm has changed, and companies must now be able to deliver products extremely fast. The entire company should be optimised for speed rather than cost efficiency. When you optimise for speed, you are able to quickly release new features that will unlock new revenue streams or at least increase customer retention. If you optimise for cost reduction, your competitors will overtake you, leaving you trailing behind.

Keeping the wrong people on too long

I believe this is one of the most critical problems that leaders face when they carry out digital transformation in their organisations. I see this over and over in every organisation that I support.

Digital transformation is a challenging process. I usually say that change is easy – unless it involves humans. During a change of this magnitude there will be many people who will lose power and influence.

I believe we should give training, coaching and above all support to everyone that will be impacted by the change. But some people will simply refuse to change and will want to continue doing the things the way they did before.

If leaders do not remove these people from the organisation, they will sabotage the change process. They will pit everyone against each other, and, even worse, they may cause good people to leave the organisation.

Lack of an organisational impediment board

When you undergo a digital transformation, most of the changes will need to be implemented by teams, and you must support them at any cost. If you implement the changes they ask for in order to satisfy the customer, you are probably going in the right direction for a successful transformation. But as we've seen, most of these changes will never be implemented because middle management will find a way to hide them from you.

This is why an organisation impediment board is so important. The team can use it to bring 'political' obstacles to the surface, allowing you to create transparency and reveal all the information that is usually hidden.

Summary

Do not delegate and silo your transformation into a PMO. Instead, reach executive-level consensus of what digital transformation represents and make it your business to understand, and agree, its aims and objectives. Involve everyone at all levels, creating and redefining roles as part of the process. Remember to interrogate the qualifications and expertise of any external consultancy you appoint. Pay attention to data and, throughout the transformation, avoid too much inward thinking. Keep sight of creating value for customers at all times.

EIGHT

Hiring Digital Transformation Partners

If your organisation is looking to appoint an external management consultancy to help with its digital transformation, where do you begin? Get it wrong and you could end up wasting valuable time and resources and still end up without a suitable solution. However, knowing what to look for will help you make an informed and trustworthy decision.

My vision is to help companies be better at what they do because my mission is to create highly rewarded, effective and efficient executives that can make an impact in the world. Elon Musk, having developed electric vehicles, says that he cares little about his competitors emulating his model because it was his mission to create an electrical-focused auto industry.[19] His ambition was to fulfil that vision. This is the same mindset that drives my own: to create a business world that is digital-age fit for the future. Executive leaders are unlikely to achieve digital transformation in their organisations on their own, especially those steeped in traditions and practices from the industrial age, and the leaders that recognise the need to adapt their thinking and daily operations along the lines I suggest frequently look to external consultants such as myself for help in creating their digital transformation strategy.

The immediate advantages are that this brings a level of neutral objectivity, free from internal politics, and the expertise to identify typical patterns that recur in almost every organisation. As much as businesses often believe that they're 'different to everyone else', over fifteen years of experience has taught me otherwise. However, when you're the executive immersed in a business you've helped to create and grow, I understand, and am respectful of, why you are fully convinced of your difference. It may well be true in terms of the products and services offered, but in terms of operations and organisation, it's rare to find an exceptional example when most businesses that need my help were designed along principles of the industrial era. The problems these principles create are what unites, not differentiates them. Once they

19 C Fortuna, 'Elon Musk's vision for the world's transition to sustainable energy', *Teslarati* (17 February 2017), www.teslarati.com/elon-musk-vision-worlds-transition-to-sustainable-energy, accessed 8 April 2021

take that leap of faith and engage external consultants, they're already demonstrating that their mindset is open to change and fresh blood. In this chapter I will examine some factors that executives need to be aware of to make informed decisions on bringing in fresh blood to their organisations from the outside.

How do you know that the consultant you're considering has the requisite practical experience best suited to your needs? If a management consultant company offers its services to help create your digital transformation, can they demonstrate that they have the five pillars you now know about in the ADAPT Methodology?® Will they be a suitable partner for you? Can you see their own digital strategy working and in place? How do they acquire their own clients? Ask them what their data strategy is and for examples of how they collect and analyse their own data. What is their product strategy and how is their company structured? If they can't supply this information, then how will they help you?

As I mentioned in the previous chapter, making the wrong decision can be as detrimental to implementing a digital transformation as doing nothing at all.

Big management consulting firms

It's easy to be tempted by the glossy brochures of the big-name, traditional management consulting firms that offer digital transformation services. It's tempting to be seduced by presentations and convincing talk – and for larger corporations (eg banks, telcos, big pharma, etc) looking to re-invent themselves in the digital era, this might satisfy their needs. They may feel reassured by the big-name reputation, but this is not always a guarantee that a consultancy has the right skill set to get the job done. Their name carries weight and the adage that 'nobody got sacked for buying IBM' has seeped into the mindset of executives, who when making a decision can rest assured that, should it backfire, they won't be fired as a result. However, my advice is to be extra cautious and carry out due diligence before finalising your decision when you hire big management consulting firms. Of course, I'm not suggesting that you not hire a large management consulting firm, just that you be extra cautious and carry out due diligence before finalising your decision. Be aware of style over substance.

Check their real-life experience

On several occasions I've been called in to rectify fundamental errors left behind in the wake of my bigger competitors who take on graduates with excellent degrees who then walked straight into a consulting position without ever having gained any practical experience. Don't get me wrong, they're smart cookies, they talk the talk, but lack the wherewithal or experience to walk the walk. Before you consider appointing a management consultancy based on its reputation, do some detective work first on the individual consultants they employ. The minimum requirement should be that they have actual, *real-life*, hands-on experience prior to working for the organisation you're thinking of hiring. It's good to say they've consulted for this or that client, but have they really got their hands properly dirty and actually done what they're going to charge you a fortune for? Before you even think of signing on the dotted line, ask to interview their nominated consultants so that you can learn about their relevant knowledge and experience.

Without a doubt, there are excellent consultants working for the bigger companies, just don't take this for granted. Being able to create a PowerPoint presentation is fine, but if that's a consultant's only experience, then look elsewhere. Ensure that your consultant has worked in an actual company, not simply in consulting firms, and has developed and implemented change as an employee within a product-led organisation, ie always 'look under the bonnet before you buy'.

Assuming the partner you're considering engaging doesn't follow my ADAPT Methodology® exactly, ask them to provide you with advance evidence of a concrete methodology or framework they have in place that will help you to achieve your own. Don't simply rely on what they show you in their brochure or on their website. Dive deep and interrogate what it is they offer carefully. This will often raise eyebrows and be met with resistance, because that's not how many of the larger firms operate, but stand your ground: you're the one that will be paying the invoices. Make sure that you've gained a full insight and understanding of their background and experience. Remember, your consultant may be filling the shoes of an executive or director and you need to be 100% confident you've made the right decision and not one based on some convincing marketing copy. Only hire a company that has a proven, clear methodology (or approach) designed to solve the sorts of problems your organisation is experiencing, or you'll fall into the trap of believing that parachuting a handful of 'expert' developers into your business will solve everything. Unless they work to a proven methodology, it won't. Anyone who begins by stating that 'each company is different, and we'll work it out as we go along' is making excuses for the fact they don't have anything to hang their hat on and they'll charge you a premium for simply winging it. The real experts will have developed a whole and proven methodology that complements their client's ecosystem and customises the solutions.

Ask for content

These days, content is a key tool that engages and acquires clients. If you've found a consultancy you want to hire, first take an in-depth look at their website. For example, any one of the bigger management consultancies might show their indisputable and excellent research findings and approaches, but they could still lack original content that sets them apart. If you can't find any material that points to original, home-grown research content such as white papers, podcasts, blog articles, subject matter books and video tutorials that explain their know-how, then ask for content. Without any such assets it's less easy to confirm their practical credentials, especially if it's not an area of expertise for your own business. In the digital era, content forms a vital component of any digital strategy, and their content should exemplify their approach to customers (as described in Chapter 1). If a consultancy is reluctant to create their own content – and make it visible – that should raise a flag in your own mind as to how they will develop your own strategy. If they're not able to educate you, how can you expect them to implement a strategy to educate your own clients?

There's no better proof of concept than a successful case study that can be backed up with a client testimonial. Success is contagious, so if you're still making up your mind whether to hire a particular management consultancy, let their previous clients do the talking for them. On the other hand, if no case studies are available, then maybe what they really excel at is great presentational skills and little else. It's also important to ensure that your potential partner can provide several cases, not just in the wider world, but also in your region or locality. Look for in your consultants what you expect your customers to look for in you.

Package deals vs daily fees

I'll stick my neck out here and state that consultants should know exactly what they're doing and how to charge a basic fee for a service-based package. I personally don't subscribe to the practice of charging a daily rate. Daily fees tell you one thing straight away – that the consultant has no idea how long it will take to implement and solve your problem. My suggestion is to search for companies that, like my own, offer a package deal that identifies the programme, the duration and the outcomes. Where a consultancy firm insists on charging a daily rate but demonstrably shows it has a defined approach or methodology then the risk is lessened, as long as it can manage your expectations by stating what the outcomes of its programme will be. An ideal basic package should include:

- Contract duration

- Methodology template

- KPIs against its timeline

- Regular reviews of progress

It shows confidence from the provider's point of view that it has a defined methodology in place and is ready to deploy all its available tools and experience to deliver.

Know what you need

You may still have doubts and concerns about which way to turn and who to work with. It may well be that you're traditionally drawn towards the notion of protecting your back by hiring a large management consulting firm as 'insurance' because you worry that a complex digital transformation is way outside of your comfort zone. Perhaps your CFO is only interested in saving costs and wants you to buy a cheap package from a tick-box exercise provider because your business revenue shrank post Covid-19, or because digital competitors are already eating heavily into your market share. Perhaps by now I've persuaded you to trust a boutique management consultant with a proven track record that will offer a more premium relationship and high-quality delivery. Before you reach any decision, it's worth summing up the three stark choices you face in selecting a management consultant firm to hire:

1. **The 'PowerPointers':** Great presentational skills, but with no hands-on experience whatsoever.

2. **The 'Big Guns':** They'll offer to take you to the moon and back but do nothing in the process. As with the PowerPointers, you might be offered a couple of days training, with a couple more

follow-up days thrown in for good measure, but that's typically all you'll get in return for your investment.

3. **Boutique consultancies:** These are the hidden gems worth digging around for. Why? Because they believe in forming close relationships with their clients and feel personally invested in the results. In an era where the world is already complex, it pays to hire a company that specialises in the digital transformation areas you're looking to problem-solve. Not only will they offer familiar tools and workshops, but they'll also offer a 360-degree, holistic approach tailored to your whole organisation, which is also a reflection of their own practice.

Summary

Once you weigh up the options, and having now read the book in its entirety, I hope you'll agree that your decision isn't simply one that comes down to money. Instead, I hope that your decision will be based on a series of informed insights in respect of where your business is today and where you think it will be next year and beyond. That's different to where you'd like it to be, because inaction or taking the wrong actions for your business can be equally disastrous for its future outlook. Knowing what you need now is a step in the right direction towards your growth and survival.

Conclusion

I hope that you are now more aware of the many and different challenges that lie ahead and that I've shone some light on the real possibilities that you, as a leader, have in your hands so that you can build and nourish your own organisation as you drive it towards the digital era. Even if your business already employs software tools as part of its core operations, you will now know that the five pillars of the ADAPT Methodology® offer you space to implement a variety of improvements:

1. **Approach:** How to acquire new customers in the digital era.

2. **Data:** Learning how to use your data to optimise your business and customer experience.

3. **Agility:** The need to build a company that can react and respond quickly to changes in the market.

4. **Product:** Developing and implementing a digital product strategy.

5. **Transformation:** Why and how the entire organisation needs to change so that it can competitively thrive in the digital era.

Each of these pillars is designed to raise your awareness of the opportunities available to transform your business in a time when the competition around you is both keen and cut-throat. That transformation will deepen your understanding of your customers and enable you to reach, react and form relationships with every one of them. It will also educate and inform your decision-making when seeking the right partners to help your journey as you move through your digital transformation. It can be a difficult road to tread, and dangerous if you happen to take the wrong steps. Our journey together need not end here. I recognise that change can be hard, but I also firmly believe that we can all learn from each other (remember the peer-to-peer communities of practice I mentioned). Of course, this being the digital era makes it even more possible to connect, no matter where we are in the world.

✔━ If you haven't yet completed the scorecard and
✔━
● ━ are still curious to know how digital-era fit your business currently is, please feel free to complete and submit it:

⊕ http://bit.ly/Scorecard_ADAPT_Book

By reading this book, you are already setting an example, placing yourself at the centre of your digital transformation. I hope this also helps reconnect you to your original passion for your business. Difficult circumstances may have forced change on both your business and the world around you, but where a darker outlook may have loomed on the horizon, I hope that what you have learned here offers a sense of real optimism for the future.

As a specialist B2B consultant, I've spent much of my time talking with leaders of organisations of all sizes and values. While identifying the main problems which prevent them from creating the digital product organisations they aim for, it's become apparent to me that there is much common ground between them. In response, and based on my ADAPT Methodology,® I have created the Digital Leadership Accelerator, an online space for company founders, C-Suite leaders, vice presidents and directors. They are invited to join me in a programme that offers them a roadmap for the digital era so that they can fulfil their potential to become successful digital leaders of the future. I extend an open invitation for you to join my Digital Leadership Accelerator and become part of a supportive, educational community where I dive deeper into the five pillars of the ADAPT Methodology.® It is also an opportunity to seek extra input and knowledge as well as share your own thoughts and ideas with like-minded leaders. Please submit your initial interest at http://digitalleader-shipaccelerator.com

Acknowledgements

I want to give special thanks to my good friend Andrea Martins, for all the support and help she has shown during the writing of this book. Thanks also to my family, who were always there supporting me in the most challenging moments.

The ideas in this book are based on several years of professional experience, gathered while working with different companies. I would especially like to thank Timo Salzsieder, Ahmed Alenazi and Mishari A Al-Assailan for trusting me throughout the years we worked together and giving me the space to try out different ideas.

Warm and special thanks to Gerard Chiva. Without him, Chapter 4, 'Product', would not have been written. My interviews with him helped me build a fantastic Product chapter.

A special thanks to José Pedro Pinto, Chief Sales Officer at BNP Paribas Personal Finance, for accepting the challenge of writing the foreword to this book.

I want to thank Alvaro Ferreira, Mário Figueira, Carlos Vaz, Miguel Moreira, Francisco Froes, Rui Negrões Soares, Rui Saraiva, Nuno Morgadinho, Fernanda Vasconcelos, José Brizida and Jorge Simões for all the ideas that we have exchanged during the past few months.

A special thanks to Rui Coutinho for inviting me to give lectures at the Porto Business School on some of the ideas explained in this book.

Thanks also to the Rethink Press team, especially Mike Elliston, for helping me create this book.

Finally, I appreciate all the support that my beta readers gave me. They provided me with valuable feedback that helped me to build a much better book. It would not have been possible without their help.

The Author

Luís Gonçalves is a founder and Chief Executive Officer at Evolution4all, a fast-growing management consulting company. In his wide international experience, he has worked in different roles, always helping companies to adapt to the digital era. Luís is currently focused on helping executives transform companies using the ADAPT Methodology.®

Contact

🌐 https://evolution4all.com

💼 www.linkedin.com/in/luismsg